AUTHENTICATE
YOUR LIFE

AUTHENTICATE YOUR LIFE

Heal, Align, And Simplify: A Journey To Authentic Living

CORI ROBERTS

Authentic Publishing
Authenticate Your Life LLC
Flagstaff, Arizona

Authenticate Your Life

Copyright © 2025 by Authenticate Your Life LLC

All rights reserved.

No part of this book may be reproduced, stored in a retrieval system, or transmitted in any form or by any means—electronic, mechanical, photocopying, recording, or otherwise—without prior written permission of the author, except for brief quotations in reviews or articles.

This book is a work of nonfiction. The events and experiences described herein are based on the author's personal insights and research. Any similarities to persons, living or deceased, or to actual events are purely coincidental unless otherwise noted.

Disclaimer

The information provided in this book is for educational and informational purposes only and is not intended as a substitute for professional advice or services. While the author has made every effort to ensure the accuracy of the information presented, readers are encouraged to seek professional guidance for their specific needs. The author and publisher shall not be held liable for any actions taken by readers based on the content of this book. Readers assume full responsibility for any choices, actions, or outcomes arising from their use of this material.

Published by Authentic Publishing
Flagstaff, Arizona

Cover design by Cori Roberts and Sage
Book layout by Cori Roberts

ISBN: 979-8-9923855-0-2

Printed in the United States of America

First Edition: April, 4, 2025

For permissions, inquiries, or bulk purchase orders, contact:
Authentic Publishing
Email: info@authenticateyourlife.com

DEDICATED TO:

To the seekers, the dreamers, and the warriors who choose to walk the path of authenticity, even when it feels impossible.

To my dad, whose love, support, and quiet wisdom remain a guiding light in my life. Your journey taught me the power of resilience, and your memory inspires me every day.

To my children: Madi, Ky and Jayden…you forever have my whole heart.

To my clients, friends, and family who trusted me with their stories and allowed me to walk beside them in their own transformations. You are my greatest teachers.

And to you, the reader—may this book be the spark that ignites your journey back to your authentic self.

With love and gratitude,

Cori Roberts

CONTENTS

A Note to You.. *ix*

Introduction... *xi*

PART 1: Laying the Foundation for Living an Authentic Life.......... 21

   Chapter 1: Core Principles for Authentication 1

   Chapter 2: Your Inner Reality Creates Your Outer Reality 9

   Chapter 3: Let's Start From The Beginning: Food as Energy 18

   Chapter 4: Frequency Tuning... 27

PART 2: Building On the Basics 41

   Chapter 5: Apply and Create Powerful Change 43

   Chapter 6: Reclaiming Your Life Force Energy 48

   Chapter 7: Preparing for a Detox 92

   Chapter 8: Plant Medicine and Psychedelics for Mental Health .. 111

About the Author.. *118*

Resources *122*

Final Thoughts *127*

References... *128*

A Note to You

Dear Reader,

Welcome to *Authenticate Your Life*.

I wrote this book for you—the seeker, the dreamer, the person who knows there's something more. Whether you've felt stuck in cycles of societal expectation, faced life-altering transitions, or simply longed for deeper connection and meaning, this book is here to guide you back to your authentic self.

In these pages, I share experiences from my personal health journey and introduce a range of tools, from advanced biohacking strategies to the simplicity of beginning with a basic detox protocol. This book is also a guide to help you reconnect with your intuition, rediscover who you are at your core, and release patterns that no longer serve you. The most important thing is to take what feels right for you (and, before implementing any practices, please consult your healthcare provider to ensure they align with your individual needs), and leave the rest behind. You may even find that one day, you'll return to this book and uncover new insights that resonate with you at a different point in your journey.

It's filled with so much information, ideas, and concepts that you can read it multiple times and learn something new each time.

As you navigate through these pages, know that you are not alone. Together, we'll explore what it means to live with courage, love, and intention in every moment. I have no doubt that our bodies are designed to find balance, heal, and transform into exactly what we are seeking. It will happen, but it will take time. For me, it took 20 years. It's a journey of unwinding the past to create the future you know is possible.

If you feel I can offer further support, please visit my website or social media for the latest updates. Even after this book is published, I continue to learn, grow, and share what I've discovered with you every step of the way. We are in this together.

Thank you for trusting me. My hope is that this book feels like a warm hug from a friend who truly sees you and believes in you.

Here's to the beautiful, messy, and extraordinary journey of becoming authentically YOU.

With love and gratitude,

Introduction

My journey began when the monotony of motherhood broke me to my core. My girls were 15 months and 3 months old and I had forgotten what sleep felt like. To survive, I created large barricades in my living room, filled with activities for my 15-month-old, because I often passed out without warning while breastfeeding.

If you've breastfed, you know about that uncontrollable passing-out phase. I'd fall asleep without realizing it, waking up 15 to 20 minutes later, disoriented, with a sleeping infant in my arms and a toddler playing noisily nearby. One day, I realized that my zest for life was gone. The endless cycle of changing diapers felt soul-crushing.

Back then, no one really talked about postpartum depression. I didn't even know what depression was. One evening at dinner, I mentioned to my husband that I didn't want to do this anymore. He asked me, "Do what?" I replied, "Life. I don't want to be here." I truly believed what I was feeling was normal. His reaction told me otherwise.

A few days later, I found myself in the doctor's office, holding a prescription bottle filled with antidepressants. The internal battle that followed ran deep. Taking the medication felt like a failure—not just to me, but to my maternal family, who were herbalists and didn't believe in medications like these. My husband, Jayson, had no issue with the idea of pharmaceuticals. It was easy for him to say, "Just take it." But for me, taking the pills felt like I was just doing what he told me to do, and that didn't sit right with me either. My heart was shattered, and I was lost and confused.

After many arguments, I finally started taking the medication. It went against everything I had ever known, but three weeks later, something shifted. I went outside and noticed how blue the sky was, how white the clouds were. I was amazed. The leaves blowing in the trees were a vibrant green—so alive and beautiful. I had never seen life in full color before. Everything had always been muted and grey.

I hadn't realized that seeing the world this way wasn't normal. How could I have? It was all I had ever known. But when you experience something new—something better—your entire perspective changes. This was my first awakening—my first glimpse that there was more to life than what I had known to be true.

As time passed, my fear of becoming dependent on the medication grew. I told Jayson, "When I find out how to feel this way naturally, I'm going to stop taking the antidepressants." That single statement set me on a journey into mental and physical health that would change my life forever and continue to guide my purpose today.

As my perception of life shifted, I opened my first business, *Holistic Waters*, where I worked as a colon hydrotherapist. I saw clients daily, listening to their stories and learning from their experiences. Clients would arrive with detox protocols and ideas about probiotics that were unheard of in 2004. Watching my clients heal themselves, I jumped in and began trying every detox imaginable, taking excessively high dosages of probiotics. I began to see my own health improve, and I knew I had to dive even deeper.

People around me often looked at me with concern because I was always on some sort of detox protocol. Looking back, I realize it was because I needed it. I was born with spinal meningitis, treated with many types of antibiotics, and continued to be on antibiotics nearly every month growing up. My nervous system was overstimulated, my gut wrecked, and my body inflamed.

Beyond the physical, I had absorbed emotional and energetic imbalances from loved ones, which embedded themselves in my body, creating even more inflammation and toxicity stored deep within my tissues. The detoxes I tried only scratched the surface. I knew something was missing. And then, as they say, when the student is ready, the teacher appears. And so she did: Dr. Michelle Hebert.

It all began because of a client who, every time she saw me, insisted, "You need to meet Dr. Hebert." At first, I resisted. I was so hesitant to take in others' advice, believing I needed to stay true to what my inner voice was telling me. But one day, I felt a gut instinct to visit her office and drop off some business cards.

The moment I walked into her office, I felt something shift inside me. My curiosity sparked. She came out to meet me, shook my hand, and took my cards. As I turned to leave, I heard a voice inside me say, "I need an appointment with her." I turned back around and asked about her services.

She handed me a list of services and prices, and my heart sank. It was more than I could afford at the time. I thanked her and started to leave again. Then she stepped out of her office and said something that stopped me in my tracks:

"I've never done this before, but I just heard a very loud message that I need to offer you my services for free until you can pay. If you can pay even a dollar, that's great. Whatever you can manage works for me. You don't need to explain—just put whatever amount under this stuffed animal."

In that moment, something shifted deep inside me. I took a breath and agreed to come in for an appointment. For my first session, I placed a dollar under the stuffed animal. Over time, as my financial situation improved, I was able to increase my donation.

It was as if my life started to flow again. Random tips from clients would go straight into my pocket and then to her. Dr. Hebert changed my life and my entire perspective on health. She opened my eyes to the connection between the subconscious mind and the physical body. She helped me understand how the stories we carry—the emotional density and unprocessed experiences—can settle in our tissues, creating misalignments and disease.

Dr. Hebert also introduced me to the concept of Crystalline Healing. In her classes, she taught us about the crystalline energy within our bodies and how to use our imagination to see it. She showed us how to recognize the density that gets stuck around it and how to listen to the messages within the crystalline energy to better understand the body.

Meeting her aligned me with my purpose. She remains one of my greatest teachers and friends to this day.

When I look back on my life, I see how pivotal moments like these alter the course of our destiny. It humbles me. It reminds me how synchronistic and beautiful life truly is.

Deepening My Connection

As I deepened my connection to my intuition, embraced detoxing, and began living with purpose and intention, my business evolved alongside me. I started integrating health coaching at the beginning of every session as a colon hydrotherapist. I realized that when clients shared their stories, I could help them identify what they were holding onto emotionally and use colon hydrotherapy as an intentional release, allowing those emotions to flow out of them. This simple shift brought profound changes to my clients.

Later, I introduced an infrared sauna to my office. Each session would begin with health and emotional coaching, followed by a colon hydrotherapy session, and conclude with time in the sauna. I taught clients the importance of learning to sweat at lower temperatures, between 102-107 degrees, which worked beautifully with infrared technology. Unlike traditional saunas, it didn't require extreme heat; instead, it trained the body to sweat naturally and was highly effective.

After a few years, I added crystalline healing to my services, filling another missing link. This process taught me the importance of integrating three critical elements: talk therapy to engage the logical mind, detoxing to eliminate the old and make space for the new, and aligning subconscious beliefs with both the logical mind and the biological body. It became a full-circle approach.

As my business continued to grow, I hired massage therapists and introduced detox body wraps, which felt incredibly fulfilling. However, a shadow side began to emerge. While I was an excellent practitioner, I struggled with the business side of things. To make matters more challenging, I was going through a divorce, raising my three children, managing three employees, and navigating a business with a shaky foundation. I had very little left to give anyone.

Eventually, I stepped away from entrepreneurship to focus entirely on my children as we worked to rebuild our foundation together.

The Next Chapter

A few years later, I felt the nudge again. As my family's dynamics shifted, I needed to find a way to support my children while maintaining flexibility. I reopened my business under a new name: Words2Wellness. To deepen my expertise, I earned my hypnotherapy certification and leaned further into the subconscious mind. My new office had two rooms: one for colon hydrotherapy and the infrared sauna, and another for crystalline healing and hypnosis.

But there was still one thing missing: I didn't know how to run a business. I thought being excellent at what I did would be enough—build it, and they will come, right? But the people didn't come to the degree I needed to support my overhead or my family. I was overwhelmed with stress, and just when I felt lost, another angel entered my life.

He introduced me to his cancer doctor, who invited me to join a holistic cancer clinic in Scottsdale, Arizona. It felt like a dream come true. In this brand-new facility, I worked alongside Dr. Cheryl Kollin, an extraordinary and ego-free doctor. Together, we collaborated on patient care, blending her expertise in cancer treatment with my mindset coaching.

This clinic was unlike anything I'd ever experienced. We had access to some of the most advanced biohacking technologies in the country. I witnessed healing from all angles—medical, spiritual, technological, and emotional. We were a dream team, but as often happens, not all dreams last. The clinic's owners had other plans, and I was let go during the height of COVID.

The Unexpected Shift

Though devastated, I was armed with wisdom, connection, and experience. As I fumbled through unemployment and supported other naturopathic doctors in the valley, another beautiful soul entered my life during a very low point. She invited me to dinner at the top of a building in Tempe. I found myself sobbing uncontrollably, spilling out my fears and frustrations.

She listened patiently and then said, "I don't know if you'd be interested, but the company I work for is hiring." Once again, everything aligned, and I found myself stepping into the world of software. As I walked to the front door of my new job, I knew this was a pivotal point of choice: to walk in as my authentic self or put on a mask and become something for everyone else but myself. I chose to try something new and be 100% authentically me. And what I learned from it is that when I was truly me, it allowed others to be themselves too. We built a department that was based on being real. We had the BEST department EVER, and thankfully, our friendships continue to flourish even after my departure from corporate.

Full Circle

As I am finalizing this book, I realize I am at another pivotal point: to be authentically myself in the world or find masks of protection. I realize that corporate was a test of whether I could be authentically me—and I did, coming out even better than I ever imagined. Now, I get to test my authentic self with the world. Terrifying, but also exactly what I need.

Looking Back

We never truly know where our future will lead us. Yet, looking back, I can see that every time I felt lost, I was eventually found, and a giant pivotal moment presented itself. Now, I feel as though I have finally arrived at my most authentic self, ready to bring two decades of experience into these pages. I am profoundly grateful to every person who has touched my life along the way, each of whom has played a part in shaping this journey.

PART 1

Laying the Foundation for Living an Authentic Life

CHAPTER 1

Core Principles for Authentication

When we embark on a health journey, it's essential to examine every part of ourselves and the world around us. Taking the time to be an observer—both inwardly and outwardly—is where transformation happens. I first encountered parts therapy during my hypnotherapy training, and it's exciting to see it gaining traction in psychiatry. In short, parts theory involves recognizing the different aspects that make up who we are (a great movie that incorporates this idea is *Inside Out* 1 & 2). As we dive deeper into parts therapy, please know that what follows is my interpretation of what I've learned and applied to deeper aspects of healing. It blends hypnosis ideology, parts theory, and the subconscious stories we carry.

> I want to highlight Dr. Frank Anderson, a brilliant psychiatrist specializing in neuroscience and trauma treatment. His work on parts theory and family systems is invaluable if you're interested in exploring these concepts further through his social media or website. He keeps his information current and relevant.

We're all complex beings, and learning to heal the individual parts of ourselves leads to greater peace and balance. Take a moment to observe yourself—whether in relationships, at work, with family, or when you're alone. Are you the same version of yourself in each scenario? Or do you wear different hats or masks depending on the environment?

Reflect on who you are at work. Picture yourself in that environment—this is one of the many 'parts' you play. Now, shift your mind to imagine yourself with your family. How different are you in that space? Or with your friends? Each of these roles represents another 'part' of you that comes to life in different settings. But let's go even deeper than that.

Let's say you were bullied as a child. That experience might still linger in your subconscious. Even though the bullying isn't happening anymore, the 'part' of you that was hurt as a child still carries that memory in your body (cellular memory). If you were to see something similar happen in your present life, like a child yelling at another child, that old wound could easily be triggered, causing an emotional reaction. In that moment, both the adult and the child parts of you would have a reaction to the present situation.

This is where healing begins—by using a current trigger to dive deeper into the subconscious and reframe the story that happened as a child. You can update it with a compassionate adult perspective. By doing this, you reclaim the power that was taken from you as a child and shift from a place of victimhood to one of strength. This is where transformation happens.

I encourage you to try this process with a manageable story from your past. Find a quiet space, and using your journal or meditation, observe a time when you felt victimized—start with something low in stress. Once you have that memory, close your eyes and imagine yourself as a compassionate coach to your younger self. Take time to listen to the part of you that was hurt. Offer compassion and understanding. Let that part know you're there for them and will always be there when needed. Continue holding space for the little you until you feel them take a breath and release the stress of the past. You'll notice a weight lifting off of you.

Often, that younger part of you will ask for a hug. When they do, use your imagination and hold them until they let go first. This process of holding your inner child and providing safety, wisdom, and trust is where many autoimmune conditions reside. Stay present with your little self until they go off and play. This is how you re-write the past to heal your future.

By reframing these old stories, you'll notice a shift not only in how you feel about your life but also in the world around you. And if you need more support, don't hesitate to seek professional help from someone who specializes in inner child work, parts theory, trauma-informed therapy, or family systems therapy. The more we acknowledge our parts, the easier it becomes to focus on healing one aspect at a time—and that healing tends to accelerate as a result.

It's important to note, especially for logical thinkers, that parts theory is not related to schizophrenia. I saw a fantastic meme the other day that said, "Healing is so hard because it's a constant battle between your inner child, who's scared and just wants safety, your inner teenager who's angry and just wants justice, and your adult self, who's tired and just wants peace... be gentle with yourself." I couldn't agree more with this meme.

Another insightful psychologist who has shaped my understanding of healing and self-exploration is Matthias Barker. His work, which is accessible and affordable, ties parts theory to relational frame theory, highlighting how the stories we tell ourselves about our past shape our behavior and actions. It's not just the trauma itself, but the narrative we've created around it that influences how we engage with the world.

The incidents we experience shape our reality, but if you're willing to reframe those stories, you can change how you see the world—and, most importantly, how the world responds to you. One simple way to reframe is by shifting the way we speak. For instance, changing phrases like "I have to" into "I get to." For example: "I get to go grocery shopping and choose meals I love" or "I get to study for a career I enjoy." Another common phrase is, "This is killing me," "This is driving me crazy," or "I can't catch a break." Words are medicine. When we use phrases like these, our bodies are listening, agreeing, and, most importantly, creating what we say.

It's crucial to be aware of the stories you tell yourself. The next time you tell a story, ask yourself: Does this story make me feel empowered and confident, or does it take away my strength? If it disempowers you, how can you rewrite the story to shift from feeling victimized to recognizing the lessons and strength you've gained? This is where parts theory can be incredibly helpful in deepening your understanding of yourself and your relationship with the world around you. Once you understand what it is you are saying, you can also ask yourself: What part of me is saying this? This takes practice and skill—to slow down, tune into your core, and ask yourself, *Which part of me is saying this?* Is it the child who needs safety? Is it the teenager who wants revenge? Or is it the adult who just wants peace?

Understanding which part of you is active allows you to lean in even more and hold space for that part. Listen deeply, repeat what that part is expressing, and offer support with compassion and empathy. Finally, ask that part of you what it needs from you to feel safe, accepted, or at peace.

I began incorporating parts theory into my coaching approach to guide clients in exploring and implementing new tools and ideas for deep, lasting change. Developing awareness of all the parts within ourselves is a vital step in this journey. Whether it's the inner child craving ice cream or the adult grappling with the weight of shifting habits, each part holds valuable insight. Every part deserves to be recognized, listened to, and supported—even when its desires or needs cannot be fully met.

Learning to hold space for all aspects of yourself is a crucial step in understanding your subconscious belief systems. By observing, listening to, and supporting these parts with compassion and gentleness, you begin to uncover who is truly in control—the logical mind or the subconscious mind. This awareness becomes the key to understanding the patterns that shape your reality and the first step toward creating lasting change.

Parts therapy is a vital component of healing because it helps us bring awareness to the subconscious—the reservoir of thoughts, memories, and belief systems that shape our perceptions and decisions. These subconscious elements are powerful because they create the reality in which you view and interact with the world. In essence, what you believe deep within your subconscious directly creates your outer reality.

But how does this happen? To fully understand, we must explore the science of energy and the idea that your words create your reality through quantum programming.

Consider the well-known phrase, "Ask, and it is given." This statement is true—but if it's so simple, why do so many of us feel that our prayers, affirmations, or desires go unanswered? The answer lies in the alignment—or misalignment—of our subconscious belief systems with what we consciously ask for.

Words are energy. When spoken, they emit vibrational frequencies that interact with the quantum field—the energetic fabric of reality. If the words you speak or the desires you project are in conflict with deeply held subconscious beliefs, that energetic misalignment prevents your intentions from manifesting. For example, you might consciously ask for abundance while subconsciously holding a belief that you are unworthy of success. This conflict creates a vibrational dissonance, blocking the flow of energy needed to bring your desires into reality.

By integrating parts therapy with an understanding of quantum programming, we begin to see how crucial it is to uncover and align those subconscious beliefs with our conscious intentions. When your inner world is in harmony, the words you speak and the energy you emit become powerful tools for creating the life you desire.

In the next chapter, we'll dive deeper into the science of words as energy, exploring how they shape the quantum field and how you can consciously reprogram your reality by aligning your thoughts, beliefs, and spoken intentions.

CHAPTER 2

Your Inner Reality Creates Your Outer Reality

When the connection between science, spirituality, and human potential is made, one name often comes to mind: Gregg Braden. His years of work bridge ancient wisdom with modern discoveries, focusing on heart-brain coherence, the power of belief, and the science of transformation. Braden's expertise reveals that we are holograms of programmable energy. He explains how the atom, being 99.99999% empty, leaves space for quantum programming—where instant miracles of healing can occur.

The empty space within the atom is quantum realm, or as I like to think of it, the God particle. Braden believes that by engaging all of your senses through the imagination of what you desire, you activate the quantum potential to remember your infinite ability to create whatever your heart longs for. Dolores Cannon shared a similar belief, teaching that when you close your eyes and imagine seeing, touching, tasting, and feeling a reality you wish to create, it's a sign that it's already present within your energy field. From there, your task is to bring it from quantum potential into physical reality—and I'll show you how.

> Side Note: The matrix within an atom is 99.99999% empty, meaning the "emptiness" contains the quantum wisdom of the universe, where every possibility exists. This emptiness, of what I like to call it the "God particle," is the energetic space that allows matter to materialize. Aligning your intention with this quantum field aligns you with the frequency needed to bring your desires into physical reality. Prayer is one way of reaching into this field—it's an act of quantum alignment and prayer. - Gregg Braden (YouTube)

Take a moment to think about what you want to create. Have you experienced fragments of this before? Often, having a reference point can help you remember what it feels like to receive. If you've never experienced it, use your imagination to picture how it would feel if it were materialized right now.

Hold the image of your desired outcome in your mind. Imagine it coming to life in the present moment. The more vivid your visualization and the stronger the feelings you attach to it, the more you align with the frequency within your body—the matrix field of infinite possibilities.

Why Aren't My Prayers Answered?

If this process is natural and always happening, why don't our prayers, wishes, and desires always manifest? The answer lies in the misalignment of the subconscious mind. Your subconscious stores memories, beliefs, vows, promises, and inherited or absorbed stories from others, all of which can block your intentions.

If the subconscious is constantly creating, you might wonder, "Why would I create painful experiences?" This connects to the idea of soul contracts—lessons your soul agreed to experience for growth. While some lessons may be premeditated, others may not. I'm still exploring this concept more deeply, but for now, we'll keep it at the surface.

To manifest what you desire, you must focus on the words you use, both consciously and subconsciously. Words are powerful tools for programming your reality. Many common phrases in the English language unintentionally signal lack or weakness. For example, saying,

"I would like to create a career that uses my talents" carries a sense of uncertainty or longing. Instead, say, "I give myself permission to create a career that uses my talents." Feel the difference?

Phrases like "I want" or "I need" signal lack to the quantum field and perpetuate that lack. Even if you say the right words, your subconscious thoughts—especially when facing challenges like unexpected bills—might contradict your intention. This inner conflict is where misalignment occurs.

Words are the command center of your energetic field—both on a micro and macro level. The challenge is that we often feel like we're saying all the right things, yet our subconscious operates on an entirely different belief system. And the subconscious is difficult to hear.

It is only in moments of silence and focused awareness that we begin to tune into it. But as soon as we try, the ego often steps in and takes control. So how do you know which voice is speaking? Is it your ego, your authentic self, or your subconscious?

In my experience, I've learned to recognize the difference. When my internal voice is afraid or focused on self-protection, that is my ego speaking. To access my subconscious, I have to step outside my ego, become an observer of my thoughts, and ask myself: Which part of me is feeling this way? My authentic self, on the other hand, speaks when I am in flow—when my thoughts and actions align with my heart.

Simply becoming aware of this—learning to recognize which part of you is speaking—is one of the most powerful ways to understand yourself.

Because the subconscious tends to retreat into the background when we focus on it, learning to observe it without force is essential. It's a skill, much like training at the gym. At first, it feels difficult and unfamiliar. But the more you create space to explore these different parts of yourself, the easier it becomes.

One of the best times to observe your subconscious is while driving. In safe, predictable conditions, your subconscious begins to take over within 10-15 minutes, allowing unfiltered thoughts to surface more freely. Recognizing when your brain shifts into an alpha state during these moments can help you become aware of your subconscious thoughts and start to rewrite the stories that arise. You don't need to close your eyes, of course, but when a thought feels out of alignment, simply ask yourself, *Do I really believe that?* If the answer is no, follow up with, *What do I actually believe about this situation?* This simple process can create profound shifts, leading to instant healing and clarity.

Although it can be challenging to tune into your subconscious when you're busy or distracted, with practice, you can train yourself to observe these thoughts in receptive moments. Learning to listen in this state is a powerful step toward uncovering and transforming limiting beliefs.

Reclaiming the Power of the Subconscious

For many, the subconscious has been portrayed as a mysterious, even dangerous place—an idea perpetuated by religion, Hollywood, and societal programming. Think of movies like *Get Out*, which depict the subconscious as something to fear. These narratives were intentionally crafted to maintain control over the masses. Imagine the shift if everyone learned to heal themselves and think independently.

When you begin to harness the power of your subconscious mind, you start to see how your inner reality creates your outer reality. The thoughts, beliefs, and emotions stored deep within you are reflected in the experiences, relationships, and circumstances that shape your life. When your inner world is aligned—filled with clarity, intention, and self-awareness—your outer reality naturally mirrors that alignment. Conversely, when your subconscious is cluttered with doubt, fear, or limiting beliefs, these inner conflicts manifest as obstacles in your external world. By understanding and transforming your inner reality, you unlock the ability to consciously create a life that reflects your highest potential. This is the bridge between science, spirituality, and human potential—the understanding that true change begins within.

Often, it's difficult for us to see what we are subconsciously creating because we are deeply attached to the world we've built. Many fear deep changes because, with transformation, a part of ourselves inevitably dies.

I recently experienced this firsthand. As I prepare to publish this book, I realize I'm stepping into a greater level of authenticity—not just within the safety of my home or personal bubble, but now, on a much larger scale, exposed to the world. Shifting into this new frequency of full authenticity means the masks I've worn for protection must fall away. And that is terrifying.

Just a few days ago, I had a full-blown anxiety attack at the thought of shedding this layer of myself. It felt as though a part of me was dying. Thankfully, a dear friend held space for me, allowing me to reflect on all the times I had previously evolved into a more authentic version of myself. Each time, I lost friends and loved ones—not because of conflict, but because, as I changed, our connections no longer aligned. I developed a deeper understanding of who I was, what I needed in relationships, and how some of those relationships had been built upon the very masks I was now shedding. In some cases, those dynamics required me to prove myself, remain defensive, or uphold expectations that weren't true to me.

So, I let go.

I released the heaviness of trying to keep others comfortable by wearing masks they loved but I didn't. And this is why many resist change—the risk of losing what they've built around them feels greater than the unknown potential of what they could create.

If you've ever tried to change or create something new for yourself but found it nearly impossible, it's often because your environment—and the relationships within it—are holding you to an outdated version of yourself.

Here's a personal example:

I lived in Tempe, AZ, for most of my life. Though I spent brief periods away, I was always drawn back. Yet, despite feeling deeply rooted there, something was always off—I just didn't understand why. As I grew older and traveled, I noticed my energy shifted dramatically whenever I left the city. I began to recognize what I truly needed in my environment to create inner harmony.

One of the biggest missing pieces for me was nature—specifically, greenery, oxygen-rich air, and a strong water element. Living in the desert was depleting. The extreme temperatures drained me, and grounding my energy into the Earth felt nearly impossible. The land beneath me was mostly solid rock, and even where there was grass, the soil was shallow, lacking depth and nourishment.

Then, last year, I was guided to move to Flagstaff, AZ. Here, the air is crisp, the Earth is rich and grounding, and the dormant volcanic energy of Humphrey's Peak has been profoundly healing. It has transformed me so much that my energy now feels as neutral and balanced as nature itself. My nervous system has healed. My mind is clear. Looking back, I see that in Tempe, I was ungrounded, constantly in fight/flight/freeze mode—and my relationships (with a few exceptions) reflected that energy.

Even though I did everything possible to ground myself, heal my nervous system, and cultivate authentic, compassionate, and available relationships, it was a constant struggle. But I couldn't fully see it until I had stepped away. It took a full year for me to gain clarity.

This is why removing yourself from what is familiar is so important—it gives you the perspective to recognize imbalances and opens the door for new possibilities. And if you can't physically leave your environment, there are still ways to shift your perspective. One powerful tool is plant medicine, which we'll explore further in Chapter 6.

For now, we're shifting from words and energy to a deeper understanding of our avatars—the human body. We'll explore its connection to energy, its role in our overall well-being, and why detoxification is essential in the journey to becoming your most authentic self.

CHAPTER 3

Let's Start From The Beginning: Food as Energy

I want to challenge you to think of food as more than just fuel for your body—consider it Life Force Energy (LFE). In his book *The Detox Miracle SourceBook*, Dr. Robert Morse explains how the energy of food can be measured in angstroms. I see this as a way to measure LFE, and I hope this concept becomes more mainstream. You'll understand why it matters as you continue reading.

So, what exactly is Life Force Energy (LFE) or food voltage? It's the amount of energy the food emits. Everything around us—your body, nature, words, thoughts, relationships—it's all energy. And so is your food.

> The idea of measuring Life Force Energy in angstroms is debated, and that's okay—new information is always evolving, and contradictions are part of growth. What I share comes from my experience, research, and over 20 years of working with clients. With the internet, you can find evidence for or against almost anything, so it's crucial to trust your intuition. Try things, see how they feel, and create your own understanding. Stay open, stay curious, and trust your inner guidance. As you grow, your beliefs may shift—and that's a natural part of the journey.

This is the core of what this program is all about. Are you ready for it? It's BIG... Here it is: **"Your energy is your new currency."** It's no longer just about the money in your pocket. The more LFE (life force energy) you have, the more your entire body comes into balance. You'll start creating from a place of attraction rather than constant grinding. A balanced life flows from balanced life force energy.

If you want to live a more authentic life, you need to understand your energy levels and figure out what boosts your energy and what drains it. Think of it like a video game—you always know your player's energy level, right? When it's low, you find ways to power up. When your player's at 100%, they can take on anything. But when their energy is low, even a small hit can take them down. It's the same in life.

Tracking your daily energy level is key to health. So, what's your energy level right now, on a scale of 1 to 10? A 1 means you're bedridden and can't move—very ill. A 10 means you're at full energy, ready to take on the world. Where do you fall today?

Dr. Robert Morse has a chart that measures the human body's energy in angstroms (LFE). He outlines the energy levels that correlate with disease and those that indicate optimal health. Check out the ranges:

Energy of Healthy Foods

- Fresh raw fruits: 8,000-10,000 angstroms
- Fresh/raw vegetables: 8,000-9,000 angstroms
- Fresh/raw milk: 8,500 angstroms
- Cooked vegetables: 4,000-6,500 angstroms

This concept is all about recognizing how the energy we consume affects our overall vitality. Let's keep exploring and growing from here.

Energy of Toxic Foods:

- Pasteurized milk: 2,000 angstroms
- Pasteurized cheese: 1,800 angstroms

- Refined flour: 1,500 angstroms

- Cooked meats: 0 angstroms (but I believe there are ways to increase the LFE of cooked meats, making meat consumption valuable for optimal health).

Body Frequencies

- Average human: 6,500 angstroms

- Cancer patients (typically): 4,875 angstroms (Morse, 2013, p. 104)

Now, let's simplify the above ranges (0-10,000 LFE). We can reduce the scale to 0 to 10. If you wake up feeling like a 4/10, it's a sign your body is more acidic and leaning toward a diseased state. This happens because, while you sleep, your body slows down, including the detoxification processes, causing stagnation in certain areas. Using tools like high-vibrational foods, proper hydration, and movement (like exercise or a vibration plate) can help get things moving and raise your energy levels. If you consistently find yourself at a lower level, don't worry—there are other tools in this book we'll cover to help with that too.

If you wake up at a 7/10, you're already operating above the average energy level for a healthy body. Now, can you imagine waking up at an 8, 9, or even a 10/10? Um, yes, please!

Start thinking about your health in terms of energy, because everything is energy—what you give, you have to replace. Let's use an apple as an example of currency.

Picture an apple growing on a tree in a beautiful organic orchard. The sun is shining, the birds are singing—it's all high-vibe energy (10,000 LFE). Let's say you pick the apple and take a bite. You feel the crispness, taste the sweetness. What's the LFE of that bite? A 10? Yeah, I think so too!

Now, what if that apple came from an overseas non-organic farm? Picture it being sprayed with pesticides, picked by machines, packaged, and shipped across the ocean. What do you think the LFE of that apple is at this point? Maybe a 6 or 7? Then it arrives at a warehouse, gets coated to extend its shelf life (Appeal), refrigerated or frozen, defrosted, and eventually lands at the grocery store. Every day it's separated from the tree, it loses LFE. By the time you pick it off the shelf, what do you think its energy is? Maybe a 3 or 4.

And don't forget—if it's been covered with chemicals or Appeal, your body has to use its own Life Force Energy to detoxify those substances.

To truly heal and upgrade our bodies, we need to focus on consuming foods that are at an LFE level of 8-10. If you're eating foods with an LFE of 2, 3, or 4, your body's energy drops to match what you're consuming (frequency matching).

What about GMO foods?

Here's how I see it in the simplest terms: God designed our planet with foods programmed to nourish our bodies. When humans alter that design through genetic modification (GMO), the body doesn't always know how to process it. It's like trying to install PC software on a Mac—it's just not made for that system. Your body might recognize and use some components of GMO foods, but the unrecognizable parts get stored in places they shouldn't, which can lead to disease.

Keeping foods in their original, natural form is key. That's why I'm not big on supplements—if we buy organic, local foods (with minimal processing), we can get all the nutrients our bodies need. But I also know that most people are inflamed, and many cannot absorb an adequate amount of nutrition from food alone. It's only when we get the body back to balance that we can live sustainably on just food. However, this idea could evolve as we lean into AI technology to analyze lab results and create new tests to understand our bodies' overall health. I believe we're in for a real treat when AI supports our medical systems with advanced testing, leading to more accurate diagnoses and individualized treatment plans.

But for now, in 2025, to create optimal health—especially when the body is in a diseased state and struggling to absorb nutrients—supplements can be crucial. This is particularly true when they serve a medicinal purpose. For example, herbal tinctures and supplements are essential when detoxing and targeting specific organs to support their natural cleansing processes. You can also get similar benefits from raw plants, but it really depends on your body—things like inflammation, genetics, and other factors come into play. No two of us are the same, and it's all about doing what's best for you, ideally in partnership with your healthcare provider.

Let's Dive into Packaged Foods and Animal Proteins

The more steps a food takes between the farm and your plate, the lower its LFE (Life Force Energy). Think about your favorite cracker. Where did its ingredients come from? Were they genetically modified? Were inflammatory oils used? How long did it sit in a warehouse? What kind of packaging was used? And how much of that cracker does your body have to detoxify, using its own LFE to process all those chemicals? Now, compare that to a homemade cracker made with raw, unprocessed ingredients. What do you think the difference in LFE might be?

I always ask myself: How much has the food been touched or altered from its original form? The more processed it is, the lower the LFE.

Now, let's talk about animal proteins like steak, chicken, pork, or fish. I like to think of them in two categories:

- **Happy animals**—cows, chickens, pigs, or fish raised in natural environments, living stress-free, eating high-vibration foods, and not separated from their babies.

- **Stressed animals**—those in overcrowded conditions, pumped with antibiotics and steroids, separated from their young, and fed a low-LFE diet.

You can already imagine the difference in LFE between these two categories.

Here's another consideration: top feeders vs. bottom feeders. Animals like pigs, crab, catfish, and oysters—bottom feeders—consume lower-LFE materials, meaning what they eat, you eat.

When it comes to animals, the quality of their lives impacts the energy in the meat you consume. If an animal is healthy, happy, and living its natural life, that higher LFE transfers to you. On the other hand, animals packed in cages, stressed, walking on their feces, and loaded with antibiotics produce meat with lower LFE. How they are killed also matters. Studies show that animals experience intense stress during slaughter, releasing stress hormones that linger in the meat. Some farmers try to mask the effects with chemicals or even soothing music, but many don't. Ingesting that stress means you're absorbing that stress hormone or energy, which leads to more inflammation.

Once the animal is killed, its LFE starts dropping immediately. If it's a high-LFE animal, it might begin at a 10, but after all the processing—packaging, freezing, transporting, defrosting, and storing—its LFE can drop significantly.

Consider the difference in LFE between meat from a locally, ethically raised animal and one from a commercial ranch. The fewer steps between the farm and your table, the better the LFE. What do you think the LFE is by the time it reaches your plate after all the commercial processing? What do you think the LFE rating of commercially processed meat would be? Now, think about the chemicals injected into the animal or even the animal's emotional state. How do you think that impacts your physical, mental, or emotional well-being?

If you're someone who feels called to eat meat, I encourage you to seek out a local farmer who raises happy animals—ones that roam free, eat natural grasses, stay with their families, and live low-stress lives. Look for a farmer who kills the animals one at a time, not in bulk. Make sure the meat is free of steroids, antibiotics, and not stored long-term in freezers. The best-case scenario is that it's fresh, in your fridge, and on your plate within a few days. Some people feel their absolute best eating meat, while others don't. Everyone's body is different. This is where your intuition is vital. Your personal health goals are nobody else's goals. I encourage you to stay curious. Even if you strongly believe one way, I suggest leaning into the flexibility of your belief system.

I personally ate as a vegan for many years to heal my gut and nervous system. For me, that was a vital part of my recovery. And now, as my body is balanced, I have brought back animal protein—and I was finally ready for it. It has shifted my health in a way I never knew was possible.

CHAPTER 4

Frequency Tuning

Everything is energy. When you consistently consume foods, books, conversations, music, and create movements all in the 8, 9, or 10 LFE (Low Frequency Energy) range, you naturally elevate to that same vibration (frequency tuning). And when your body operates at such a high frequency, disease cannot survive. But when LFE drops, disease finds room to grow.

This principle is reflected in nature. Imagine a flowing, vibrant river—its energy is at a 10. The plants and wildlife around it are thriving. Now, think about the stagnant water in the corners of the riverbank—what grows there? Harmful bacteria and other things that can make you sick. The same happens in your body. It's essential to keep your body moving with high-LFE foods, drinks, thoughts, actions, people, environments, and really...your entire reality.

Quick thought: when your body becomes stagnant, your digestion often slows down too. If your bowels aren't clearing daily, that's when bacteria, yeast, and parasites start to thrive, just like in the stagnant parts of a river. When your bowels slow, your entire elimination system—lymphatic system, kidneys, and liver—begins to stagnate. If this isn't addressed, inflammation sets in, and mucus is produced to help move things along. If the mucus isn't eliminated quickly, it can create an environment where diseases can thrive. The body needs to stay in constant motion—your bowels, kidneys, and lymphatic system all need to keep moving to maintain health. I'll dive deeper into this when we discuss detoxing and how to keep your body moving. But the most important thing to remember? Don't let your bowels become stagnant.

We've established that the time it takes for food to go from farm to table is crucial for maintaining a high LFE. How food is handled also plays a role in its energy. If food is altered from its natural form—with chemicals, medications, or genetic modifications—your body has to use its own LFE to detoxify it. We can't forget the emotional health of the animal, either. If the animal was stressed, anxious, or depressed, that energy is passed on to you. Lastly, the length of time food is processed also impacts its LFE.

Let's rethink how we approach grocery stores and learn how to shop differently. A good rule of thumb is to stick to the outer walls of the grocery store—this is where you'll find the highest-vibrational foods (highly processed meats and dairy being exceptions). The more processed foods are usually found in the center aisles.

Dairy can be tough on the body, and there's a good reason for that. Even if it seems like a better option than something like a cracker, it actually requires more energy to digest for many individuals. This is because dairy has an extra layer of fat (called a fat globule) around each milk molecule. That layer makes dairy harder to digest, requiring additional enzymes or stored energy to break it down. And even when your body manages to digest it, dairy naturally leads to mucus production. So, if you find yourself feeling congested—whether in your ears, nose, or throat—after eating dairy, that's why. Where there's stagnant mucus, there's inflammation, and with inflammation comes a higher risk of harmful bacteria and disease that will find the mucus as a home to hide and reproduce.

Goat's milk, on the other hand, is a little easier for the body to handle. Its fat globules are thinner, making it easier to digest. Plus, raw dairy—before it's pasteurized—contains loads of nutrients that pasteurization destroys. Alternative milks are a good option, but I'd steer clear of store-bought ones. Instead, invest in a nut milk maker and make your own. It's easy, and you control exactly what goes in—nothing more, nothing less. Now, let's dive into all the layers of food allergies and sensitivities. I love this part because when I made these connections, it felt like my whole world shifted.

How Do Food Sensitivities and Allergies Develop?

Here are a few common causes:

- **Genetics**

- **Blood type**—Did you know different blood types break down food differently? I highly suggest looking into this to learn more.

- **Chronic inflammation in the gut**—Caused by stress, alcohol, medications, acidic foods, and more.

- **Emotions**—Yes, emotions are linked to food sensitivities, too.

Let's dive a little deeper into how emotions play a major role in food sensitivities.

Our emotions and subconscious stories play a huge role in how we react to certain foods. The subconscious mind records every moment of our lives, starting in the womb. It's like the black box on a plane, keeping track of everything down to the millisecond. This is great when we're recalling positive memories, but when it comes to trauma, it's a different story. Trauma gets stored in our subconscious (cellular memory of our physical bodies) and can trigger emotional and physical responses, even when we don't realize the root cause. For more on this, check out *The Body Keeps the Score* by Dr. Bessel van der Kolk, a Dutch psychiatrist and trauma researcher, which explores the deep connection between trauma and the physical body.

As we work through our emotional triggers, rewriting the stories that no longer serve us, we can heal on a deep cellular level, raising our energy and improving our overall health. Here's an example of how emotions can influence food sensitivities:

Let's say when you were two, your mom gave you a bottle of milk, and you felt so happy, relaxed, and at peace. You'd sip on the milk, watching her sing and hum while she cleaned the kitchen. Everything felt perfect—until someone barged in, starting an argument. The calm, peaceful vibe instantly shifted to tension, and the energy in the room went from soothing to chaotic. Normally, this might not have a lasting effect, but when this scenario repeats—milk paired with extreme stress and fear—it leaves a deep subconscious imprint.

Babies are like little sponges, absorbing all the energy around them. In that moment, your tiny body picked up on the stress, becoming tense and upset, even without fully understanding what was happening. Your subconscious began linking milk with those feelings of stress and fear. The more it happened, the stronger the association became, eventually programming the subconscious to believe that milk was something to be afraid of or indigestible… something you 'couldn't digest or understand.'

Reflection:

Do you have certain foods you just don't like? Take a second to think of one. Close your eyes and imagine trying to eat it. What feelings or thoughts come up when you think about it?

Now, use those feelings to ask your subconscious: when was the first time you felt this way about that food? Close your eyes and visualize the scene—who was around you? What was going on that made this food feel so unpleasant? It's not the food itself; it's the memory tied to it that your body holds onto.

Once you identify that memory, ask yourself: are you ready to let go of it and create a new relationship with this food? If the answer is yes, what would you want the new story around this food to be?

Whenever you notice foods that carry an old story, you can work through this by doing some inner child work or simply setting an intention to rewrite the narrative. Try eating the food with a positive affirmation and visualize pulling that old memory out of your body. Imagine it like an old cassette tape, pulling the old story out and replacing it with something new. It may sound a little out there, but your thoughts shape your reality. If you believe in the change, it's real—regardless of what anyone else thinks.

Anytime you feel resistance—whether with food or anything else—ask yourself when the first time was you felt that resistance. Let's lean into what resistance might feel like:

Resistance can feel different for everyone, but generally, it shows up as a sense of discomfort, tension, or hesitation. Some common ways resistance might feel:

- **Physical tension:** Tightness in the chest, shoulders, stomach, or jaw. You might feel like you're holding your breath or clenching muscles without realizing it.

- **Emotional discomfort:** Anxiety, frustration, irritation, or even anger. You might feel unsettled or uneasy about something but can't quite pinpoint why.

- **Mental blocks:** Procrastination, distraction, or avoidance.

Resistance often shows up as excuses or a feeling of not being ready to face something, even if it's something you want or know you need to do.

- **Fatigue or lethargy:** Sometimes resistance can manifest as a heavy, drained feeling where you lack energy or motivation to move forward.

- **Overthinking:** You might find yourself stuck in a loop of doubts, fears, or "what-ifs," which keeps you from taking action.

- **Feeling stuck or trapped:** It might feel like you're up against an invisible wall, unable to push past something, or like you're spinning in circles without progress. It can feel like a pushback from your mind or body, keeping you from fully engaging with whatever it is you're trying to do or experience. It's often a signal that there's something deeper going on beneath the surface—fear, limiting beliefs, or unresolved emotions.

When you find resistance, decide if you want to keep holding onto that story or if it's time to let it go. You can do this with everything that triggers you. Those triggers are actually doorways to healing on the deepest level. The more time you spend understanding and rewriting these stories, the more you can heal.

Resistance is a Golden Opportunity for Healing

Resistance is one of the greatest indicators of where healing is needed. The feeling of resistance is not a barrier—it's a doorway to deeper transformation. When we push resistance away, it doesn't disappear; instead, it continues to manifest in different ways until we address it. If we resist, it persists.

The best approach is to acknowledge resistance the moment you notice it. Pause and identify the authentic feelings that have surfaced. Find a quiet space, close your eyes, and become an observer of these emotions. Instead of reacting, simply witness them.

As you tune in, ask yourself: Which part of me is speaking?

- Is it the inner child, who is afraid and seeking safety?
- Is it the adolescent, who is angry and longing for justice?
- Is it the adult, who simply desires peace?

Once you identify which part of you is active, lean in and listen. Why do they feel the way they do? What do they need?

Then, gently coach yourself:

- If your inner child is speaking, offer reassurance and safety.
- If your adolescent self is demanding justice, acknowledge their pain and work together to find resolution.
- If your adult self feels trapped in an old story, ask: Is this belief still true for me? If not, get curious—what new perspective or story would bring you harmony and peace?
- By engaging with resistance in this way, you turn it from an obstacle into a powerful guide toward self-awareness and healing.

One example we talked about earlier was waking up and feeling low-LFE. That feeling can also show up as resistance. When you wake up, ask yourself, *What am I resisting in my current situation?* Are there things I feel I 'have to' do but don't feel aligned with? If you had a magic wand, what would you want to change in that moment? What is the resistance trying to show you? Lean in and learn from your resistances—they are an important part of your healing journey.

Let me share an example from my own life about subconscious programming and food sensitivities—it was a total game-changer. For years, I lived in a constant state of fight or flight, which eventually led to autoimmune issues, thyroid problems, adrenal fatigue, chronic pain, and exhaustion. Every doctor I saw put me on adrenal support supplements, and I took other things to manage the symptoms. Whenever I was under a lot of stress, my symptoms would flare, and I'd go back to the supplements.

Then one day, I went to a doctor who also practiced applied kinesiology. She tested me for all the supplements I was taking, including the adrenal support. When she tested that one, my body rejected it. I was shocked.

Why would my body react to something that's supposed to be good for it? That's when everything clicked for me. Even though something might be 'good' for us, our subconscious has its own story. In my case, it had started associating my adrenal supplement with stress, and my body began to resist it instead of benefiting from it. What was supposed to help me actually started triggering a stress response, making me sensitive to it.

From this experience, I learned the importance of switching up my supplements after finishing each bottle. By doing this, I kept my subconscious from attaching emotions or stress to them, almost like tricking it to avoid the same programmed responses. I realized we've created subconscious stories around every food and supplement we consume. So now, when I eat, I pay attention to the messages my subconscious is sending. What am I telling myself about this food? Do I still want to hold onto that story? The power to create health lies in our thoughts, intentions, and what we choose to consume—not just food, but media, people, and experiences too.

Here's another story that might resonate. I had a client who had a unique relationship with coffee. While many people think of coffee as something that can deplete the adrenals or add acidity to the body, for her, it was something entirely different. Her story around coffee made it therapeutic. Yes, therapeutic.

Years ago, a client told me, *"Cori, I know I'm supposed to give up coffee, but I loooooove it! It brings me so much joy."* So I leaned in. I wanted to know more about her association with coffee. My programming is: coffee is acidic and overstimulates the nervous system and adrenal glands, so if your system isn't balanced, I usually recommend avoiding it—or at least prepping your body to handle it better. But as I listened to her story, coffee was tied to family, connection, and love. She grew up in Oregon, where coffee was a part of heart-to-heart conversations and gatherings with loved ones. Because of this, I saw it as a positive, therapeutic tool in her life, though I did suggest she limit it to 6-8 oz and add a pinch of baking soda to reduce the acidity if needed.

The key, though, was in her awareness. I advised her to be 100% present when drinking her coffee, focusing on the love, connection, and healing it represented for her. If she ever found herself using coffee as just a stimulant, we'd need to address the underlying issue. Why was she feeling depleted? What had drained her energy so much that she needed that extra boost?

And hey, I'm human too—we all need an extra push sometimes, and that's okay. There's no judgment, just a need for awareness and an honest, gentle conversation with yourself. That's where the healing begins.

It's crucial to remember that whatever you truly believe, your logical mind and your subconscious mind need to be aligned for real change to happen. Your body will always act on what your subconscious believes. Even if, logically, you know something to be true, if your subconscious believes otherwise, that's the belief that wins out. That's because your subconscious controls 90% of your belief system. So, yes, beliefs can be tricky—your mind might say one thing, but your subconscious can pull you in a different direction.

Let's say you're excited to do something big in your life—like taking a vacation to a place you've always dreamed of. Just thinking about it fills you with inspiration. You talk to others, and that excitement grows. Your vibration rises as you imagine yourself going. But then, a few days later, the guilt creeps in—worries about the money being spent, or fears about stepping outside your comfort zone. Do you feel that conflicting energy? At first, you were all in, seeing the trip as something expansive and beneficial. But as the idea settled, it hit deeper layers of your subconscious, where old programming kicked in, creating conflict. Suddenly, the fear or guilt gets louder than the initial excitement, and you either cancel the trip or push it off for "another time."

In this situation, I'd encourage you to find a coach or therapist who understands the layers of logic and deep-rooted subconscious programming. They can help you dig into the stories tied to that fear or guilt, allowing you to gain a higher understanding of why you believe certain things deep down. Once you see the bigger picture, you can make decisions from a place of awareness, recognizing all the parts of you that are playing a role. That's when you can start rewriting the stories that no longer serve you, releasing yourself from the past and bringing you fully into the present moment.

PART 2

Building On the Basics

CHAPTER 5

Apply and Create Powerful Change

Everything is energy. Our thoughts, conversations, the food we eat, our homes, work environments, relationships, phones, TV, podcasts, music—everything around us carries energy. Becoming aware of how these elements impact your life is key to reaching optimal health.

Side Note: Throughout this section, I'll invite you to engage in activities and jot down reflections. These prompts are designed to give you space to explore your thoughts—whether in the moment or whenever you feel ready.

As we prepare to make powerful changes in your life, it's important to take time to reflect on how each of these concepts impacts your journey toward becoming your authentic self:

- Becoming conscious of your subconscious thoughts and programming

- Recognizing the different parts of you that surface in various situations

- Tuning into your LFE (Life Force Energy) number (1-10) in every moment

- Identifying high-vibrational foods at the grocery store

- Understanding the emotional programming behind your food choices

- Uncovering your personal food stories

- Noticing how resistance shows up in your body, learning to identify which part of you is resistant, and getting curious and compassionate as you coach that part of you back to who you are today.

Creating optimal health isn't about following a diet—it's about embracing a lifestyle. That's why we'll take things slowly, making small yet meaningful changes that bring you into alignment with your authentic self.

We'll begin by breaking down your life into energy—identifying what builds your Life Force Energy (LFE) and what depletes it. And the first place to look? Your phone and social apps.

How can we shift your phone from being an energy drain to an energy booster?

Social apps like Facebook, Instagram, Telegram, and TikTok are a part of modern life, and that's okay. But let's detox your phone so you can use it with intention—rather than letting it consume your energy.

First step: Awareness

What's your intention when you pick up your phone? What's the first thing you check, and why? Now, let's make your phone more aligned with your energy. Start by changing your background to something that brings you joy or reflects what you're working toward. When I want to manifest something in my life, I create a background with an image or affirmation that reminds me of my goals. For example, I've written affirmations on sticky notes, taken a picture, and used that as my phone background.

Next, simplify your home screen.

I have only eight apps on mine—just what I need to stay connected with my kids and clients: text, calendar, clock, appointment calendar, call, email, search engine, and music.

Go through your apps and delete as many as possible. You can always reinstall them later if needed. Then, create folders for the remaining ones. This way, you'll feel a sense of calm as you move through your phone.

Turn off notifications.

Get rid of any app that displays red numbers or icons begging for your attention. You already know which apps are important for staying connected. Those notifications are designed to distract you and keep you glued to your phone longer.

Now that your phone is simplified, take a moment to close and reopen it. How does your body feel? Less overwhelmed? That simplicity is exactly what your body needs.

Next, let's talk about social apps.

I get it—we need social apps for business and staying connected with loved ones, and that's totally fine. But it's still important to keep them as simple as possible. For example, I've turned my Instagram into something that feels like a magazine. If I were flipping through a magazine, what would I want to see? Only positive images, motivational quotes, and updates from family and friends I truly care about.

I manage four different social media accounts—each with a clear purpose. Three are for business, and one is for personal and family connections. Two accounts focus on my photography, where I share my work; one is for Words2Wellness, where I uplift and share knowledge; and my personal account is where I post content I want my kids and future generations to know about me. Every account serves a specific purpose. My Facebook has become more like my LinkedIn, but a little more personal. When I was going through a tough time, I would post at least three photos daily—something that brought me joy. Setting an intention for each app helps keep my focus clear and my content aligned.

Being intentional with each app is key—not just with what you post, but with what you consume. I strongly recommend following accounts that inspire, uplift, and motivate you. Remember, what you take in shapes who you are. If a post makes you feel off or unsettled, hit unfollow. And if it's a family member whose content triggers you, it's perfectly okay to unfollow. You might need some support navigating any backlash from doing so, but your well-being comes first.

I suggest unfollowing 3-5 accounts every day. Simplifying your digital space is essential for healing and maintaining your energy. There's also a handy feature on most social apps—muting. If you don't want to unfollow or unfriend someone, you can mute them, and they won't be notified. This way, you can protect your peace. Social platforms change all the time, but no matter what, the goal is the same—let go! The more you release, the better you'll feel.

If you're feeling brave, delete the app altogether.

If you really need to access it, make it a little harder—like only from your computer. Trust me, there's something freeing about deleting an app and reclaiming your time.

CHAPTER 6

Reclaiming Your Life Force Energy

Energy Leaks, Subconscious Attachments, and Releasing Emotional Cords

Now that we recognize ourselves as creators of energy, it's important to understand that everything we think, say, and do sends out a vibration into the universe. In return, we experience physical manifestations that reflect our internal reality. Beyond conscious creation, however, our subconscious patterns and energetic imprints play a major role in shaping our reality—sometimes in ways we don't even realize.

Did you know your energetic body can develop energy leaks without you even being aware of them?

The energetic body serves as the bridge between your physical, emotional, and spiritual selves. It is the unseen force that governs vitality and well-being. While modern science typically focuses on the physical body, holistic healing traditions acknowledge that humans are multidimensional beings, existing simultaneously in physical, emotional, energetic, and spiritual states.

The energetic body acts as a translator between these layers, ensuring that what happens in one aspect of our being impacts the entire system. For example, unprocessed emotions can stagnate as energy, leading to physical discomfort, chronic fatigue, or illness. On the other hand, when the energetic body is clear and flowing, the physical body feels strong, the emotional body stays balanced, and the spiritual body opens up, bringing clarity—whether through meditation, journaling, or connecting with nature and loved ones.

Energy Leaks: Where Is Your Life Force Energy Going?

Energy leaks occur when unresolved emotional experiences continue to run in the background of our subconscious, quietly draining our Life Force Energy (LFE). These experiences hold significant emotional weight because they remain unprocessed, causing us to unknowingly expend energy keeping them alive.

Our ego plays a key role in this. It stores these unresolved experiences as a self-protection mechanism, believing that by holding onto past pain, it can recognize similar situations in the future and prevent us from experiencing them again. However, instead of protecting us, this mechanism often backfires, keeping us stuck in a fight/flight/freeze state, where our nervous system remains hyper-vigilant, prioritizing survival over peace.

Understanding and healing these energy leaks is essential for reclaiming your vitality and freeing yourself from subconscious cycles of fear and resistance.

Energy Drains Through Relationships and Environments

Another way energy leaks occur is through our connections to certain people and environments. Individuals or places with low Life Force Energy (LFE) often tap into the reserves of those with stronger LFE, slowly depleting them.

We've all experienced moments where we feel great—only to leave a certain place (like a crowded mall, a concert, or an office) feeling completely drained. That's because you were energetically depleted.

Even in close relationships, this happens frequently. As parents, we intuitively feel our children's emotions—even when they're far away. This is because we are energetically attached to them, just as we are to those we love.

People in abusive relationships often get their energy drained by their partner, which lowers their LFE and can even lead to disease. In my years of coaching cancer patients, I've noticed a strong correlation between narcissistic abuse and the other partner developing cancer or other chronic illnesses. Reclaiming your energy and pulling it back from all the places it's been scattered is crucial to fully healing the physical body. Let's start exploring ways to reclaim your LFE (Earthing, Biohacking Technology, Bodywork, Therapy/Coaching, and Sleep).

But while all relationships involve energetic exchanges, some replenish us, while others drain us. The key is identifying which relationships support your well-being and which ones pull you into cycles of depletion.

The Cost of Holding Onto Unhealthy Attachments

Relationships—especially with family—play a major role in our overall health. Society has conditioned us to believe we must maintain relationships at any cost, especially within families. But at what point does that cost become too high?

Some people remain so entangled in family dynamics that they fail to recognize how these relationships negatively impact their health. Holding onto old obligations out of guilt, fear, or duty creates energy leaks that deplete our Life Force Energy. Letting go, setting boundaries, and consciously choosing relationships that align with our highest path allows us to cultivate authentic, nourishing connections instead of draining ones.

Healing does not come from attaching to others for love, validation, or identity. It comes from reconnecting to the infinite source of energy—

God, the Divine, or your Higher Self. When we release the belief that someone outside of us must complete us, we reclaim our sovereignty.

As we strengthen our connection to Source, we stop relying on external validation for our sense of peace. Instead, we begin to trust life's intelligence, allowing us to move through the world with greater ease, confidence, and flow.

How Subconscious Attachments Form in Relationships

Every relationship we form creates energetic cords of attachment—some are healthy and life-giving, while others are draining and restrictive.

For example, consider the mother-daughter relationship (though this applies to all relationships). A mother may subconsciously project expectations onto her daughter, thinking, *Since you're MY daughter, you should be* _____, *you should do* _____, *and you should think* _____. The daughter, in turn, absorbs these projections as truths about herself, creating energetic cords of expectation.

Likewise, the daughter projects onto her mother, thinking, *Since you're MY mom, you should be* _____, *you should do* _____, *and you should think* _____. These unspoken energetic contracts become embedded in the subconscious minds of both individuals, shaping their behaviors and relationship dynamics.

Over time, these projections blur the lines between who we truly are and who others expect us to be.

To untangle this, ask yourself:

"Do I truly believe this, or have I absorbed someone else's idea of who I should be?"

If the answer is no, visualize yourself pulling that belief out of your body and releasing it. Then, consciously replace it with what you do believe.

This dynamic also occurs in friendships and romantic relationships. Think of your best friend. Now fill in the blanks:

"Since you're my best friend, you should _____, you should _____, and you should _____."

See how easy it is to project expectations onto others? These etheric cords exist between us and everyone we've ever formed a deep connection with—past lovers, friends, family members, and even jobs or homes. But should these people (or things) carry our projections?

No.

They deserve to be exactly who they are, just as you deserve to show up authentically in your relationships. If an attachment is based on expectation rather than true connection, it may be time to reevaluate the relationship.

Cutting Energetic Cords & Clearing Energy Leaks

If a relationship is draining your energy, it's your responsibility to:

1. Release your projections.

2. Love the person exactly as they are.

3. Let go of the relationship if it no longer serves your highest good.

No one owes anyone anything except to be authentically themselves.

Have you ever left an interaction feeling completely drained? That's because the person may have projected their energy onto you or attached an etheric cord to your field. Etheric cords are unseen energetic connections that form between people, places, objects, and even past experiences. These cords act as conduits for emotional, mental, and spiritual energy, *transmitting* feelings, thoughts, and vibrations between individuals. Etheric cords allow us to tap into the energy of others—mostly on a subconscious level—enabling energetic exchange, telepathic communication, or even attachment to people, places, or things. Some of these cords are healthy and supportive, while others can be draining or disruptive.

One meditation practice I routinely do before bed is setting the intention for my higher self or God to cleanse my energetic field, releasing or cutting any cords of attachment that are not in my highest well-being or that of others. Keeping your energy clear in relationships—whether with loved ones, coworkers, or anyone you interact with—is essential for maintaining emotional, spiritual, and energetic balance.

Here's the key: no one can drain your energy without your subconscious agreement.

This is why setting strong energetic boundaries is essential.

When we don't release subconscious contracts and energetic attachments, they linger in the background, quietly draining our energy. But when we begin cutting cords and sealing energetic leaks, we reclaim our vitality, inner peace, and strength—allowing us to fully embody and express our most authentic self.

Final Thoughts: Clearing the Path for True Healing

True detoxification isn't just about cleansing the physical body—it's about releasing old energetic attachments and simplifying where your energy is going.

By consciously cutting cords, setting boundaries, and choosing relationships that energize rather than drain you, you create a life that is aligned, peaceful, and deeply fulfilling.

Because, at the end of the day, peace is the goal—and when you clear your energy, you make space for exactly that.

Did you know you might have been born with less LFE than others?

If a mother is depleted while carrying a child, her body taps into the baby's resources to keep herself strong and ensure the baby's survival. This means some of us are born already running on low energy reserves.

This concept extends beyond the womb. Science now shows that trauma, diet, and stress don't just affect one person—they can be passed down through generations.

The Science of Inherited Trauma: Epigenetics

Dr. Rachel Yehuda, a leading expert in epigenetics, has conducted extensive research on how trauma can have intergenerational effects. Her studies suggest that traumatic experiences can lead to epigenetic changes—modifications in gene expression that do not alter the underlying DNA sequence—and may be passed down to subsequent generations.

One of her notable studies focused on the children of Holocaust survivors. Yehuda and her team discovered that these offspring exhibited epigenetic alterations in the FKBP5 gene, which regulates stress. These findings indicate that the trauma experienced by the parents led to biological changes inherited by their children, influencing their vulnerability to stress-related disorders.

Further research by Yehuda has explored how trauma is transmitted across generations. She has proposed that epigenetic mechanisms may be responsible for conveying trauma from parents to offspring, including developmental programming during pregnancy and changes in germ cells before conception. These insights reveal how trauma affects not just individuals, but their descendants as well.

Yehuda's work highlights that while genetic predispositions play a role in our health, environmental factors and personal experiences can significantly influence gene expression. This view offers a more dynamic understanding of genetics, emphasizing the potential for change and adaptation across generations.

In summary, Dr. Yehuda's research provides compelling evidence that trauma leads to epigenetic modifications that may be inherited. This underscores the importance of considering both genetic and environmental factors when addressing the long-term impacts of trauma (Yehuda et al., 2015).

Our genes can turn on and off based on our environment, mental state, and lifestyle choices. Meditation, prayer, nutrition, and everything we're working on here can rewrite these patterns and help heal inherited trauma.

The Connection Between Emotional Trauma & Physical Detox

For years, I've observed patterns in detox—both in my own healing and with my clients. I could see how emotional trauma stored in the body affected physical health, but science didn't seem to explain what I was witnessing. Recently, I came across a podcast featuring Gregg Braden, and his explanation finally connected the dots for me. For more on Gregg Braden's podcast, scan this QR code:

How Emotional Trauma Stores in the Body

Every experience and emotion creates a chemical reaction in your body, producing something called a neuropeptide. Neuropeptides are chemical messengers released in response to emotions. Joyful experiences allow them to flow and metabolize naturally, but when we experience something we can't process or integrate (like childhood trauma), these neuropeptides remain trapped in the body's tissues and organs.

This survival mechanism allows the body to hold onto unprocessed trauma until we're ready to heal. However, the body doesn't distinguish between trauma from an hour ago or 60 years ago—it perceives it as the same.

Neuropeptides themselves aren't toxic, but when they remain stagnant, they disrupt the body's natural balance. Over time, they attract toxins and inflammation, creating blockages that slow circulation and hinder the body's ability to detoxify properly. This stagnation weakens the immune system, making the body more vulnerable to illness and disease. As unprocessed neuropeptides accumulate, they often contribute to chronic pain, fatigue, and dysfunction in the areas where trauma has been stored. If left unaddressed, this biochemical congestion can lead to long-term physical and emotional imbalances, reinforcing cycles of discomfort and dis-ease.

Your body is always working to heal you, but it's essential to give it the tools to release these stored emotions and toxins.

Healing isn't linear, and it's easy to fall into the trap of blaming ourselves when our physical, mental, or emotional health takes a dip. But I hope this chapter has helped you see that there's much more at play than what's visible on the surface.

Our soul contracts, genetics, environment, traumas (both past and present), and daily experiences all shape our health and energy levels. Add in work, school, relationships, and the emotional weight of everyday life, and it's a lot to process.

But here's the empowering part: You have the power to change your narrative.

Looking ahead, the work you do today will not only transform your own life but also shape the emotional and physical health of your children, grandchildren, and generations to come. That's why we do this deep, inner work—it's not just for us. It's for the future.

Energy as Currency

Every choice we make in the present moment shapes our future selves. Imagine you're out with friends, enjoying a couple of glasses of wine. In that moment, you feel great—your energy spikes from a 4 to an 8 or even a 9. But what happens the next day? Your body has to work overtime to detoxify the alcohol, pulling from your energy reserves. Instead of waking up feeling recharged, you might find yourself back at a 3 or 4, running on depleted energy.

This is the nature of energy exchange—your Life Force Energy (LFE) is your life's currency. If you constantly spend more than you replenish, your cellular batteries drain, and over time, this impacts your physical, mental, and emotional well-being.

For optimal health, you want to consistently operate in the 7, 8, 9, or 10 range of LFE. That's why being mindful of how you invest your energy is crucial. Highly sensitive individuals—such as empaths and introverts—often require more recovery time because they naturally give more of their energy away. The key is to understand your own energy rhythms and recognize when it's time to pause, replenish, and recharge.

Reconnecting with the Body After Trauma

For many, especially those who have experienced trauma, survival has meant disconnecting from the body. Reconnecting can feel foreign, even frightening, especially if dissociation has been a long-standing coping mechanism. However, true healing requires returning to the body—fully inhabiting it rather than observing life from the outside.

Disconnection often stems from trauma, stress, or chronic illness, where the body begins to feel like an enemy—something unpredictable, untrustworthy, or even painful to exist in. As a result, individuals may mentally or emotionally check out to avoid the discomfort. This survival response may help in the short term but can ultimately lead to feeling ungrounded, numb, or detached from the present moment.

Healing involves more than just returning to the body—it requires creating safety within it. When we are disconnected, we lose access to the body's innate wisdom and become more vulnerable to external energies. Reconnection, then, is about establishing a relationship with the body rather than feeling trapped in it. This is why I like to use the term *avatar*—it shifts the perception of the body from something restrictive to something we can consciously engage with and nurture.

Several techniques can support this reconnection, including breathwork, grounding, biohacking technologies, bodywork, coaching/therapy, and developing strong sleep patterns. These practices not only strengthen our connection to the body but also recharge our cellular batteries—and fully charged cells are essential for manifesting your dream life.

Now, let's explore each of these healing modalities in more detail.

Square Breathing & Grounding Exercise

Here's a simple yet powerful practice to help regulate your nervous system: Square Breathing.

Another technique I often use—with both clients and myself—is reassuring the nervous system that you are safe. The goal is to realign your mind and body with safety and presence through repetition and intentional breathwork, allowing your nervous system to shift out of fight/flight/freeze mode.

Grounding Through the Safety Mantra

If you're feeling stuck in a fight/flight/freeze response, try this:

1. Lie down somewhere safe—on a bed, in a quiet space, or even in your parked car.

2. Place one hand on your sacral chakra (just below your belly button) and the other on your heart.

3. Close your eyes and take deep, steady breaths.

4. Repeat this mantra: *"I am safe. It is safe to be in my body now."*

5. Keep repeating the mantra until you feel an emotional release. If tears come, let them flow. Continue until you feel fully grounded in your body.

When you're outdoors, take your shoes off, connect your feet to the Earth, and continue practicing the mantra. Over time, as you deepen your connection with your body, you'll also begin to attune to the energy of the earth. Your Life Force Energy (LFE) will expand, and you may notice a shift—colors will appear more vibrant, sounds will become clearer, and a profound sense of oneness will emerge. I highly suggest walking barefoot on raw Earth daily.

Healing Trauma & Rewriting Your Path

Trauma can disconnect us from our true selves, often trapping us in cycles that make it hard to create lasting change. Why? Because our internal reality shapes our external experiences.

When trauma imprints on the nervous system, it keeps us locked in fight/flight/freeze. Even if we consciously desire transformation, our subconscious is still running an outdated program—rooted in fear, survival, and past pain. This is why breaking the trauma cycle can be so challenging. But it is possible. It just requires patience, courage, and the willingness to take small steps.

For me, an unexpected realization came once I had healed my body and was no longer in pain. Instead of feeling free, I fell into another depression. Strange, right? But looking back, I now understand why. When I was in pain—physically and emotionally—it gave me a direction. That suffering became my fuel, my obsession to uncover the secrets of healing, not just for myself but for others too.

And when the pain was gone, I lost my purpose.

Which made me wonder: Do we unconsciously create health crises or mental imbalances to give ourselves a sense of purpose? My purpose is to serve—to lift, support, guide, and unconditionally love others for the unique beings they are. And I wouldn't have discovered that without the pain of my past—without my struggles with depression and health challenges. So, what if the very thing that feels unbearable in your life right now is actually the doorway to your purpose?

Even though trauma can pull us off our path, it also has the potential to redirect us toward alignment—if we allow it. The key is finding a trauma-informed therapist, coach, or guide who can help you move through the trauma, rather than staying stuck in it. That's where the magic happens.

Healing isn't about erasing the past—it's about integrating those fragmented parts of ourselves, harmonizing the energy of our experiences, and realigning with our authentic self. When we shift from survival mode to creation energy, everything begins to align, and we move into flow.

Then, one day, you look up—and your dream life is right there. It was always there. But when trauma clouds your energetic field, it filters your perception, allowing you to see only the pain within you. When you heal, those filters dissolve. And suddenly, the world you've been longing for reveals itself—it was waiting for you all along.

Biohacking Technology: Optimizing Your Energy

There are countless machines designed to boost Life Force Energy (LFE)—some are highly effective, while others are less so. The key is doing your research, consulting with your healthcare provider, trusting your intuition, and experimenting. There's no right or wrong here—if you try something and don't notice a difference, that's okay. It just wasn't the right fit for you.

Some of my favorite biohacking technologies include the BioCharger, PEMF-Pulse XL Pro, the Harmonic Egg, and Rife machines. I recommend searching for wellness centers or practitioners in your area that offer these devices and giving them a try. As biohacking evolves, more advanced tools will continue to emerge. The important thing is to stay curious and observe how these technologies affect your energy. Did they increase your LFE, or did you feel neutral? Sometimes, the benefits aren't immediately noticeable, but months or even years later, you may find they've made a significant impact.

Understanding PEMF & Cellular Energy

The more I explored biohacking, the more fascinated I became with cellular voltage and frequency for health. I've become a total nerd about it! For example, when I was in pain, I'd use the PEMF machine in my office, and within 20 minutes, my pain would be reduced by half—sometimes gone completely. Here's the simplest way to understand Pulsed Electromagnetic Field (PEMF) therapy:

Imagine every cell in your body as a tiny battery—37.2 trillion microscopic batteries. These cells constantly release energy to perform their functions. However, when a cell is damaged, it drains energy from neighboring cells, and if it's not recharged, it malfunctions or dies (think "zombie cells"). Just like our phones need daily charging, our cells do too.

A PEMF machine acts as a charging station for your body. While you simply lie there, electrical currents help restore energy at the cellular level. Just as high-vibrational foods fuel your body, these machines offer another way to replenish your energy stores.

For reference:

- A healthy person's LFE ranges between 6,500 to 10,000 angstroms.
- Someone with cancer typically has an LFE around 4,875.

These biohacking technologies help restore and elevate those levels, supporting cellular health and vitality.

BioCharger: Frequency & Energy Transmission

Another favorite tool of mine is the BioCharger, which emits healing frequencies through the air. If you hold a light bulb while the BioCharger is running, the frequency alone will cause the bulb to light up—just from the energy passing through your body.

I've personally used the BioCharger to support my lymphatic system and overall cellular health. Sometimes, I'd leave a session feeling energized, while other times, I'd experience detox symptoms and feel depleted—which is completely normal. Hydration is key when using any biohacking technology, as water acts as a conductor, allowing frequencies to communicate better with your cells.

Nature: The Ultimate Energy Source

While technology is powerful, the most sustainable and bio-identical energy source is nature itself. Everyone connects with nature differently—that's your unique medicine. For me, it's dense jungles, waterfalls, monsoons, the ocean, and mountaintops—places where I feel completely recharged.

Intimacy as Energy Medicine

Another powerful way to recharge your energy field is through intimacy. This can be through:

- Connection with a partner (touch, communication, vulnerability, lovemaking)

- Solo self-care (taking a bath, reading an uplifting book, swimming naked, sensual touch, self-pleasure)

Deep intimacy—whether with yourself or another—allows your most vulnerable, authentic self to be seen and loved, restoring emotional and energetic balance.

Exercise: Moving Energy in Alignment with Your Needs

Exercise is another way to recharge, but it's important to find what works for your body. When I was sick, exercise drained me. I even trained for and ran half marathons because I was told it would help—

but I was miserable the entire time. Eventually, I realized running wasn't my way of recharging.

For those with chronic illness, pushing too hard can do more harm than good. Instead, I focused on:

- Meditation

- Clearing my mind

- Eating high-vibrational foods

- Supporting my detox pathways (liver, skin, lymph, kidneys, colon)

I also worked with energy healers, acupuncturists, and therapists to maintain balance. Even if you're dealing with chronic illness, movement remains essential—it just might look different from traditional exercise.

For some of my closest friends and clients, exercise and strength training are essential for their mental health, acting as a key source of energy and stability. Everyone's needs are different. Put me in a gym, and my nervous system contracts—but put me on a mountain to climb, and my energy expands. Learning what truly supports and energizes you is vital. Your body thrives when you honor what feels natural and aligned with your unique rhythm.

Home Biohacking Tools

For at-home use, two of my favorite tools are the Mini Theragun and the LifePro Waver Mini Vibration Plate. The Mini Theragun is excellent for stimulating deep muscle energy, helping to release tension and improve circulation. Meanwhile, the LifePro Waver Mini Vibration Plate works wonders for activating the lymphatic system and encouraging the body's natural detoxification process.

A fun fact: If you notice itching while using a vibration plate, it's a sign that stagnant lymph is finally moving! This is a great indication that your body is starting to flush out toxins. To enhance the detoxification process, try using a lymphatic brush before or after your session to further support lymphatic drainage and overall circulation.

Infrared Saunas: Deep Cellular Detox

Another go-to biohacking tool is the infrared sauna. While more businesses are offering them now, it's important to understand how infrared benefits your health. Infrared light is part of the natural spectrum of sunlight, but our eyes can't see it. Interestingly, our organs produce their own infrared light—but when an organ is struggling, its infrared output decreases. Other organs then try to compensate, leading to imbalance.

This is why sunlight feels so good—our bodies instinctively crave infrared light to restore balance.

If you're considering buying an infrared sauna, keep these things in mind:

- Look for ceramic heating tiles (for even light distribution)
- Ensure glass windows are covered (infrared escapes through glass, reducing potency)
- Use the sauna naked (infrared cannot penetrate clothing)

Unlike traditional steam saunas, infrared saunas work best at lower temperatures. The goal isn't just to sweat—it's to gently detox the body.

I keep mine at 105°F and start sweating within 8-10 minutes. And not just a light sweat—I'm talking full-on "just got out of the pool" sweat.

If you don't sweat easily at lower temps, you might have congested sweat glands and need to use the sauna more frequently to get things moving. It's okay to start at a higher temperature to stimulate sweating, then lower it once stagnation clears.

Cold Plunging & Brown Fat Activation

When exposed to cold water, the body immediately begins working to generate heat and maintain core temperature. This process activates brown fat, triggering the release of norepinephrine, a neurotransmitter that enhances energy metabolism and fat oxidation. As brown fat works to warm the body, it burns calories and increases overall metabolic efficiency, making cold plunging a powerful tool for fat loss, energy production, and cellular resilience.

Brown Fat, Cold Plunges & Longevity

Research shows that individuals with higher levels of brown fat tend to have lower body fat percentages, improved metabolic function, and better cardiovascular health. Because brown fat activation is associated with reduced inflammation, enhanced glucose metabolism, and better circulation, cold plunging is increasingly recognized as a key practice for longevity and overall vitality.

Pairing cold plunging with regular exercise, proper nutrition, and infrared sauna therapy can further enhance brown fat activation, maximizing its benefits for fat burning, metabolic health, and cellular optimization. By integrating this practice into your routine, you can strengthen your body's adaptive response, improve endurance, and support long-term health and resilience.

Bodywork: Supporting Your Energy Field

Another essential tool for boosting cellular energy is bodywork, including:

- Massage
- Craniosacral therapy

- Myotherapy

- Polarity therapy

- Reflexology

- Energy healing

When you're diving deep into your authentic self-journey, these therapies offer support, relief, and something to look forward to.

Biohacking offers endless tools for optimizing your Life Force Energy (LFE). The key is exploration—testing what resonates, what elevates your energy, and what feels best for your unique body. Stay curious, stay open, and most importantly—trust your intuition.

For more information about cold plunges and brown fat activation, please scan this QR code:

Therapy/Coaching

Mental health support is equally important on your healing journey. As you detox and become more aware of your resistances, past traumas, and health challenges, having a strong support system is essential.

I recommend scheduling at least one weekly session with a therapist, hypnotherapist, counselor, or transformational coach. An outside perspective is invaluable when you're working to rewrite your inner narratives. Often, we don't realize what's possible until someone helps us see new perspectives and opportunities.

If you're ready to dive deeper into reprogramming your subconscious to align with your current intentions, I highly recommend working with a transformational coach who also specializes in hypnotherapy and has trauma-informed training.

Here's why:

Recently, I had a session with a client in which we followed my two-hour approach—first hour dedicated to talk therapy/coaching, and the second hour focused on hypnosis and intuitive channeling. This session reminded me of the powerful impact of in-person sessions.

During our conversation, my client shared an experience from her time staying with her parents in San Francisco. She described an emotional heaviness so intense that it kept her bedridden for nearly two days. As we talked, I remembered that she's very sensitive to energies and easily attuned to her surroundings. I suspected that she might have been picking up on the chaotic energy in San Francisco, particularly the turbulence related to homelessness. We both connected over this and discussed ways she could protect her energy while traveling.

However, when we moved into the hypnosis and channeling phase, a completely different story unfolded. The energy in the home was heavy with unresolved grief—lingering from those who had lived there before.

Her subconscious revealed that she had made soul contracts and vows to help a family member carrying immense grief. Every time she entered the home, she unknowingly absorbed and transmuted that energy, clearing the space—yet it drained her in the process (this is another way our energy can deplete without us realizing why). As we explored further, we noticed cords of attachment connecting her to this family member, actively draining her energy. On a soul level, she had vowed to help. But the question arose: Did she still want to uphold these vows, or was it time to rewrite them?

Ultimately, it's not our job to heal others—healing is an individual journey. When we attach ourselves to someone else's healing process, we risk depleting our own energy and creating imbalance. The belief that "since you're my (best friend, mother, father, sibling, etc.), you should ____" is a projection of our own unhealed wounds. Others are not here to fill the gaps in our souls—that's our work to do, in partnership with the Divine. When we take ownership of our wounds and actively heal them, we step into true personal sovereignty.

However, this concept can be difficult to integrate culturally. Many of us inherit subconscious obligations passed down through our lineage, conditioning us to believe we're responsible for carrying the pain of others. Learning to set boundaries around this can be challenging, but it begins with simple self-inquiry: What can I do in this situation? And what am I unable to do? Understanding your personal limitations when helping others is crucial.

Each of us faces countless demands on our energy, which is why understanding your "yes" and "no" is vital. And when you need to say no, it doesn't have to be a dead end—you can offer alternative suggestions for how to help in a way that aligns with your well-being. The outdated idea that we must sacrifice ourselves for others needs to be redefined. We must honor our energetic boundaries so that every interaction comes from a place of authenticity.

Imagine your overall energy level is an 8, and someone asks for your help. Since your reserves are high, offering support feels effortless and fulfilling. But if you're operating at a 3 or 4, giving more energy could leave you even more depleted. In those moments, it's important to be honest about your capacity. A simple, compassionate response might be:

"I'm feeling really depleted right now. Let me take a couple of days to recharge, and then I'll check in with you to see how I can best support you."

This way, you honor your energy while still offering support in a sustainable manner. Setting boundaries isn't about withholding love—

it's about ensuring that your love and energy come from a place of wholeness, not depletion.

Finding the Right Practitioner for Your Healing Journey

As we've seen, the logical mind and the subconscious often prioritize different things. While your mind might focus on one area of healing, your subconscious might direct your attention elsewhere. That's why finding the right practitioner, coach, or healer is so important—someone who can help you bridge that gap and guide you to deeper self-awareness.

So, how do you find the right person to support you?

Building a strong relationship with yourself and your body is key. Your body picks up on energy much faster than your mind, which is often filtered through past experiences and beliefs. Your body doesn't filter—it simply senses. That's why sometimes you just *know* things, even when you can't logically explain why.

Steps to Finding the Right Practitioner

1. **Start with a Referral** – Ask a trusted friend or respected person for recommendations.

2. **Do Your Research** – Check out their website and social media. Do their values and beliefs align with the type of healing you seek?

3. **Listen to Your Body** – As you read about them, pay attention to how your body feels. Do you feel curiosity, excitement, or peace? Or do you feel resistance? Trust those signals.

4. **Schedule a Consultation** – Many practitioners offer 15-minute introductory calls. During your consultation, ask about their approach and note how your body responds in their presence. Do you feel safe, heard, and accepted? Most importantly, ask yourself if you believe they can help you. Trust your intuition—your body often knows before your mind does. If the connection feels right, go ahead and book your first session. If not, keep searching until you find someone who truly aligns with your needs.

Committing to the Process

Sometimes, finding the right fit takes time. But trust your instincts during the first session—you'll know if it clicks. If it does, I recommend committing to at least 4-6 sessions over 2-3 months to allow for meaningful progress.

If something feels off, don't hesitate to keep looking until you find someone who truly resonates with you.

Manifesting the Right Practitioner

Prayer and meditation can help streamline the process. After meditating, when your energy is clear, set an intention for the type of therapist, coach, or guide you need. Ask your higher self, guides, and God to help bring that person into your life. The right practitioner will appear.

I personally offer 1:1 coaching and group mentorship through my membership program. Each session is virtual, but everything I share in this book reflects the practices I use in my own life and in my practice. If you feel aligned, please visit my website and social media pages for more information. My mission is to help others reconnect with their authentic selves—just as I continue to do in my own journey.

Sleep

Not long ago, there was a cultural push to glorify getting only 4-5 hours of sleep a night—as if less sleep equaled more success and productivity. The "hustle mentality" of sleeping less and hustling more cracks me up. I even questioned if something was wrong with me because I've always needed more sleep to fully reset my nervous system.

The truth is, for our bodies to properly heal and restore balance, we must cycle through different brainwave states—gamma, beta, alpha, theta, and delta. Each stage plays a vital role in recharging cellular energy and supporting overall health. If you're not getting deep, restorative sleep, your body isn't fully resetting for the next day.

One way to better understand your sleep cycles is by using a wearable tracker, such as the Whoop band. While technology continues to advance, I've found this tool to be incredibly effective in measuring sleep quality, recovery, and nervous system balance.

The Traditional Chinese Medicine (TCM) Organ Clock

In Traditional Chinese Medicine (TCM), there's a concept called the "Organ Clock," which connects specific times of the day to different organs and their functions. Each organ has a two-hour window during which it is most active—working to repair, detoxify, and replenish energy. This cycle is tied to the flow of "Qi" (life force energy).

Understanding this rhythm can offer insights into sleep patterns, energy fluctuations, and even emotional imbalances. Here's a breakdown of the Organ Clock and what each time period represents:

- **7 AM – 9 AM: Stomach** → Optimal digestion time—this is the best window to eat a nourishing breakfast.

- **9 AM – 11 AM: Spleen** → The spleen supports energy production and nutrient absorption, so staying hydrated and eating high-quality foods is important.

- **11 AM – 1 PM: Heart** → The heart's energy peaks, making this a time of heightened activity and vitality.

- **1 PM – 3 PM: Small Intestine** → The body continues to digest and absorb nutrients, supporting sustained energy.

- **3 PM – 5 PM: Bladder** → Associated with fluid metabolism and waste elimination.

- **5 PM – 7 PM: Kidneys** → A time for replenishing vital energy and balancing stress levels.

- **7 PM – 9 PM: Pericardium** → Linked to emotional well-being and connection, making it a great time for relaxing or socializing.

- **9 PM – 11 PM: Triple Burner (San Jiao)** → Supports hormonal balance and prepares the body for sleep.

- **11 PM – 1 AM: Gallbladder** → Aids in digestion and detoxification. Waking up during this time may indicate anger or difficulty making decisions.

- **1 AM – 3 AM: Liver** → The liver works hard to detoxify the body. Waking up at this time may indicate stress, frustration, or toxin buildup.

- **3 AM – 5 AM: Lungs** → This is when lung function and respiration peak. Waking up during this time may indicate emotional grief or sadness.

- **5 AM – 7 AM: Large Intestine** → The body prepares for elimination, making this the best time for a morning bowel movement. (Vermes, 2020)

Understanding this clock can shed light on why you wake up at specific times during the night or experience energy dips throughout the day. I recommend using it as a tool for self-inquiry. When you feel out of alignment, take note of the time and reflect on whether there's a connection between the corresponding organ, its emotional associations, and what you might be processing subconsciously. This awareness can help you identify patterns and guide you toward deeper healing.

Your Energy & Sleep Needs

Each of us has unique energy needs when it comes to achieving optimal health. Not everything I've shared will resonate with everyone—and that's perfectly okay.

The key is to identify what truly replenishes your energy. Whether it's making jewelry, painting, fixing things, crocheting, gardening, or walking through the trees, prioritize activities that recharge you. Pay close attention to how you feel during and after each activity to better understand what nourishes your mind, body, and spirit. Keeping a healing journal or personal energy dictionary can be a powerful tool. Write down the practices that bring you clarity and balance so that when life feels overwhelming and your perspective becomes clouded, you can revisit your journal and remind yourself of the steps that have previously guided you back to alignment and inner peace.

Unburdening the Mind and Body: Awakening to Your Authentic Truth

Healing can feel overwhelming, especially when we consider all the layers of being human—ancestral energy (epigenetics), environmental toxins, emotional and physical trauma, subconscious programming, relationships, and the daily stressors of life (like grocery shopping). It's easy to get lost in the complexity of it all. But what if the path to authenticity isn't about adding more, but about simplifying—removing the density that has accumulated over lifetimes? When we lighten these burdens, we gain clarity, flow, and alignment.

We've discussed detoxing the emotional body, but an equally important aspect of releasing burdens is physically detoxifying the body.

If you search online for information on detoxification, you'll find conflicting opinions—some articles claim that detoxing isn't necessary. In an ideal world, this might be true. If we lived in a pristine environment—free from pesticides, radiation, airborne chemicals, and industrial pollutants—our bodies would naturally detoxify and maintain inner harmony with ease. If our diet consisted solely of organic foods grown in nutrient-rich soil, and we lived on a farm where animals were raised ethically and sustainably, our bodies would efficiently cleanse themselves without additional support.

However, the reality is far from that. Modern life exposes us to an overwhelming number of toxins—from processed foods and chemically treated water to pollution in the air, artificial lighting, and everyday household products laden with synthetic chemicals. The very materials in our furniture, flooring, and cars release toxins into our environment, contributing to a constant influx of stressors that our bodies must work tirelessly to process.

Because of this increased toxic load, our bodies require additional Life Force Energy (LFE) to effectively detoxify and purify our cells. On top of that, genetic factors, such as the MTHFR gene mutation, can further hinder the body's natural detoxification process—meaning some people struggle to eliminate toxins as efficiently as others. And as medical advancements continue, we're likely to discover even more genetic variations that affect detoxification pathways.

So, while it's true that detoxing wouldn't be necessary in a world untouched by modern pollutants, we don't live in that world. Given the conditions of our environment, detoxification must be a deliberate and integral part of maintaining overall health.

Physical Toxins Bind to Emotional Trauma

From the moment we're born, we're exposed to chemicals, and over time, we accumulate them in our bodies. While our bodies are designed to naturally eliminate toxins, this process doesn't always function as efficiently as it should. We each carry genetic weaknesses passed down through generations, and some of us are born with weakened adrenal glands from the start. Recent studies show that when a mother experiences high levels of stress and has low-functioning adrenal glands during pregnancy, she may draw on the baby's resources to maintain the strength needed to carry the pregnancy to term.

Weak adrenal glands can trigger a ripple effect in the body, impacting systems like the hypothalamus and pituitary gland. This can lead to hormone imbalances that disrupt metabolism, blood chemistry, and overall physical and emotional health. Terms like adrenal fatigue, leaky gut, chronic fatigue, fibromyalgia, and autoimmune diseases have become more common, but doctors don't always know exactly what's happening. These terms often serve as catch-alls for a variety of symptoms.

Detox: At Its Core, It's About Simplifying

We live with so many moving parts, but the more we can simplify our body, mind, and spirit, the more peace, gratitude, and energy we'll experience. When you let go of everything except what's most important, what remains? A life that's fully present and ready to be lived. When we're weighed down by physical toxins, emotional baggage, and stress, we end up feeling overwhelmed, irritable, and exhausted.

How the Body Naturally Detoxifies: A Complete Breakdown of the Detox Pathways

The human body is constantly working to detoxify and eliminate waste to maintain balance and optimal health. Every moment, it filters toxins, breaks down metabolic waste, and removes harmful substances that could lead to illness, stagnation, or inflammation. The primary detoxification organs—the skin, lungs, bowels, kidneys, and liver—work together to eliminate waste. One of the most overlooked yet essential components of detoxification is the lymphatic system. According to Dr. Robert Morse, the lymphatic system acts as the body's drainage system, ensuring that toxins do not accumulate and cause congestion.

Detoxification is not a passive process; it requires the proper function and support of these organs to keep elimination pathways open. When one or more of these systems becomes sluggish, toxins begin to back up and recirculate, leading to fatigue, inflammation, bloating, skin conditions, and chronic disease. Understanding how each detox pathway works—particularly the lymphatic system—allows for deeper healing and cellular regeneration.

The Skin: The Body's Largest Detox Organ

The skin plays a significant role in elimination. Often referred to as the body's "third kidney," it helps expel toxins through sweat. When the kidneys are not filtering properly, the skin takes on the extra burden, resulting in conditions like acne, eczema, psoriasis, or excessive body odor. Sweating is one of the most effective ways to remove toxins stored in fat cells, which is why practices like infrared sauna therapy, hot-cold showers, and dry brushing can help support detoxification through the skin. Avoiding chemical-laden personal care products and hydrating with structured water further enhances the skin's ability to eliminate toxins.

The Lungs: Clearing Waste Through Respiration

The lungs are another vital detoxification pathway, expelling carbon dioxide and volatile toxins through respiration. Shallow breathing, a common result of stress, can cause a build-up of metabolic waste, reducing oxygen flow to the tissues. Deep diaphragmatic breathing helps move the lymphatic system, as it depends on movement for circulation—unlike the circulatory system, which is pumped by the heart. Practices like breathwork, aerobic exercise, and reducing exposure to air pollutants are essential in keeping the lungs clear and supporting detoxification.

The Bowels: Final Exit for Digestive Waste

The bowels serve as the final exit for digestive waste. When elimination is sluggish, toxins remain in the colon too long and are reabsorbed into the bloodstream, leading to bloating, brain fog, and systemic inflammation. A healthy colon should eliminate waste regularly, ideally after each meal. Dr. Morse teaches that many chronic health issues stem from lymphatic stagnation, which directly affects digestion. When the lymphatic system is congested, waste isn't properly drained, leading to a toxic buildup in the intestines. To prevent stagnation and support detoxification, maintain a fiber-rich diet, undergo colon hydrotherapy, and avoid processed foods.

The Kidneys: Filtering the Blood

The kidneys play a crucial role in filtering the blood and removing water-soluble toxins. Dr. Morse emphasizes that most people's kidneys are not filtering properly, leading to lymphatic congestion and toxic buildup. When the kidneys fail to eliminate waste efficiently, toxins accumulate in the lymphatic system, causing widespread inflammation, joint pain, adrenal fatigue, and water retention. Proper hydration with structured spring water, kidney-supportive herbs like dandelion and nettle, and reducing dietary stressors (such as excessive protein) help restore kidney function. Dr. Morse suggests monitoring urine for sediment—visible particles indicate that the kidneys are successfully filtering waste. Short-term dry fasting can also help reset kidney filtration and enhance detoxification.

The Lymphatic System: The Body's Sewer System

The lymphatic system is the body's primary waste management system, responsible for filtering out toxins, dead cells, bacteria, viruses, heavy metals, and environmental pollutants. While detoxification also occurs through the skin, lungs, bowels, and kidneys, these organs rely on the lymphatic system to transport waste for elimination. As Dr. Robert Morse describes, the lymphatic system functions as the body's "sewer system," ensuring toxins do not accumulate in tissues.

Unlike the circulatory system, which is powered by the heart, the lymphatic system has no pump of its own. It depends entirely on movement, hydration, and diet to function properly. When lymphatic flow becomes sluggish, toxins get trapped in tissues, leading to chronic inflammation, autoimmune disorders, swelling, and fatigue.

How the Lymphatic System Works

The body contains two primary fluids: blood and lymphatic fluid. Blood delivers oxygen and nutrients to every cell, while the lymphatic system removes cellular waste. After a cell absorbs what it needs, it releases toxins and metabolic waste, which are transported through the lymphatic system, passed through lymph nodes, and ultimately filtered out by the kidneys. If the kidneys aren't effectively eliminating waste, congestion occurs, creating a toxic backlog that can manifest in various health issues.

How to Keep the Lymphatic System Healthy

Because the lymphatic system doesn't circulate on its own, daily movement is essential for keeping it active. Rebounding on a mini trampoline encourages lymphatic drainage, while yoga and vibration therapy enhance circulation. Dry brushing before showering stimulates the lymphatic flow by promoting detoxification through the skin. Alternating between infrared saunas and cold plunges further supports circulation, while lymphatic massage or Electro-Lymphatic Therapy (ELT™) can help release stagnation and encourage the movement of trapped toxins.

Nutritional support also plays a key role in maintaining lymphatic health. Dr. Morse recommends raw fruit juices, such as fresh concord grape juice (with seeds), which act as natural astringents to pull toxins from lymphatic tissue and aid in elimination. In addition to fruit, herbal remedies can help break up stagnation, improve lymphatic flow, and reduce toxic buildup, further supporting the body's natural detoxification process.

Supporting the Body's Detoxification System

Detoxification is not about targeting just one organ—it requires a holistic approach. When one detox pathway becomes blocked, toxins attempt to exit through other routes, often leading to symptoms like skin breakouts, sinus congestion, digestive disturbances, or inflammation. True detoxification happens at the cellular level, requiring lymphatic movement, kidney filtration, and proper hydration to support waste removal.

By optimizing all elimination pathways, the body can naturally clear toxins, reduce inflammation, and regenerate at a deep cellular and energetic level. Detoxification is not just about cleansing—it's about restoring flow, reconnecting with the body's innate healing intelligence, and laying the foundation for long-term vitality. When given the right tools—such as structured or spring water, nutrient-dense foods, movement, herbal support, and emotional and spiritual support—the body has the remarkable ability to heal itself and return to a state of balance.

CHAPTER 7

Preparing for a Detox

The Detox Journey: What to Expect, How to Prepare, and Making It a Lifestyle

Detoxing is more than just removing toxins from the body; it's a deepening of your connection to your mind, body, and spirit. It's about shedding old energy, emotions, and habits that no longer serve you. The deeper you go, the more you'll realize that detoxing is not just a physical process—it's an awakening to your authentic self.

Detoxes often create heightened sensitivity. Being around others may feel overstimulating, and you may crave solitude as your body and mind process the changes. This is normal, and it's important to honor that space. As your body begins detoxing, you may experience temporary fatigue, headaches, flu-like symptoms, skin flare-ups, or digestive changes as your body eliminates toxins. Old injuries may also feel inflamed. These symptoms are all signs of healing, indicating that your body is actively working through physical and emotional layers of your past.

The Emotional Side of Detox

In Traditional Chinese Medicine (TCM), emotions are deeply linked to specific organs, and imbalances in these organs can manifest as both physical symptoms and emotional disturbances. Understanding these connections helps identify and address both emotional and physical health concerns.

- **Liver:** The liver is associated with irritability, mood swings, bitterness, anger, and resentment. Over time, chronic frustration or suppressed anger can generate excessive heat in the liver, which manifests as migraines, high blood pressure, red eyes, dizziness, and even sudden outbursts of rage. To support liver health, practices like Tai Chi, Qi Gong, deep breathing exercises, herbal tinctures, hydration, and consuming sour or bitter foods—such as lemons and green apples—can help keep the liver flowing.

- **Heart:** The heart's divine emotion is joy, but it can also create anxiety and restlessness when out of alignment. In TCM, the heart plays a vital role in emotional balance. When the heart is imbalanced, symptoms like insomnia, palpitations, nervousness, and difficulty speaking clearly may arise. A balanced heart promotes inner peace and emotional resilience. Meditation, laughter, meaningful connections with loved ones, and avoiding overstimulation can help maintain heart harmony.

- **Lungs**: The lungs are closely linked to grief, sadness, and depression. As the organ responsible for breath and the intake of Life Force Energy (LFE), they serve as a gateway for processing and releasing emotions. When grief becomes stagnant, one might experience shallow breathing, chronic fatigue, asthma, or frequent colds. Crying is a natural mechanism for emotional release and lung healing. To support lung health, breathwork, spending time in fresh air, and releasing suppressed emotions are essential.

- **Spleen**: The spleen is associated with worry, concern, overthinking, and obsessive thoughts. It plays a crucial role in digestion, both physically (transforming food into LFE) and mentally (processing thoughts and emotions). Excessive worry can weaken the spleen, leading to digestive issues, bloating, fatigue, and brain fog. To strengthen the spleen, consuming warm, nourishing foods like root vegetables is beneficial. Grounding activities and mindfulness practices can also help calm an overactive mind and support spleen function.

- **Kidneys**: The kidneys are deeply connected to fear, insecurity, and willpower. They govern deep-seated emotions related to survival and resilience. When kidney energy is depleted, it can lead to chronic anxiety, adrenal fatigue, lower back pain, premature aging, and reproductive issues. In contrast, strong kidney energy strengthens courage, determination, and endurance. To maintain kidney health, it's essential to reduce stress, ensure adequate rest, and consume mineral-rich foods like seaweed and bone broth.

- **Stomach:** While closely linked to the spleen, the stomach is affected by anxiety, nervousness, and emotional overwhelm. Digestive distress, such as nausea, acid reflux, and bloating, often stems from emotional tension. Stress eating or a lack of appetite during periods of anxiety can signal an emotional imbalance affecting the stomach. Practicing mindful eating, reducing stress, and avoiding excessive stimulants can help regulate stomach health and restore digestive harmony.

In TCM, emotional and physical health are interconnected, and imbalances in one area can affect the entire system. Suppressing emotions can lead to physical ailments, while processing them in a healthy way supports overall well-being. Healing approaches such as acupuncture, herbal medicine, dietary therapy, Qi Gong, and emotional release techniques can help restore balance, allowing both body and mind to function optimally.

Detox Preparation is Critical

Taking time to prepare for a detox—2 to 3 weeks before starting—is vital in creating a solid foundation. This ensures you have all the tools necessary to move through all stages of the detox process. Every time I've jumped into a detox or seen clients do so, 99% of the time, it hasn't been successful. It usually ends early, or corners are cut just to get through a rough spot.

Proper preparation is key. Choose dates for your detox that don't conflict with parties, celebrations, or gatherings. Add supportive activities like massage, biohacking, and transformational coaching to help you navigate when emotions arise. Equip yourself with tools like journaling, movement, breathwork, or grounding exercises to move through difficult moments. Proper preparation greatly strengthens your ability to complete your detox.

Letting friends and family know about your detox ahead of time can help create a supportive environment rather than facing resistance. Schedule self-care activities—massages, therapy, or time in nature—to assist with emotional releases. Journaling your intentions before you begin can provide clarity on what you hope to clear and create. Building a support system is essential, whether it's joining a detox group, working with a coach, or simply having a friend to check in with.

When detoxing, if emotions aren't fully processed, they may return to the tissues for later resolution. Over time, unresolved emotions can contribute to chronic inflammation, cysts, or disease. That's why true detoxing must address not only the physical body but also the mind and spirit.

Reconnecting With Your Inner Voice

One of the most profound aspects of detoxing is learning to tune in to your inner dialogue. We've been conditioned to ignore this internal voice, yet it is one of the most crucial elements of becoming your authentic self—and, most importantly, living wholeheartedly as you. Detoxing provides an opportunity to reconnect with yourself, break free from past conditioning, and create a more aligned, empowered version of who you truly are.

In my years of holding space for individuals on their healing journey, I've found that many have unconsciously disconnected from their emotions as a means of survival. Some struggle to identify what they are feeling at all, while others have an intricate vocabulary of emotions. Understanding what emotions feel like and learning to name them is a powerful step toward self-awareness. When you take the time to create your own "dictionary of emotions," you begin to give voice to the parts of yourself that have long been silent.

Unhealed emotions are often buried—not because they are irreparable, but because, at the time, you lacked the tools to hold space for yourself during deeply emotional experiences. Detoxification allows these emotions to resurface, offering you the opportunity to meet them with awareness, understanding, and compassion. This is where true transformation happens—when you finally acknowledge, process, and integrate the parts of yourself that have been waiting to be heard.

Detoxing is full of layers, and one detox will not do the trick—it just scratches the surface. Detoxing is a lifelong practice. Just as you wouldn't clean your home once and expect it to stay spotless forever, the body requires regular detoxification. We are constantly exposed to toxins from food, water, air, furniture, cars, plastics, fabrics, stress—practically everything around us. Giving your body rest and support is more necessary now than ever before in human history.

Choosing the Right Detox for You

Finding the right detox begins with understanding your "why." What is your intention?

Do you want more energy? Are you looking to heal emotional wounds? Are you aiming to deepen your connection with yourself? Do you want to focus on a particular organ (gut, liver, kidneys, lymphatic system, heart, connective tissue, etc.)? Or are you simply looking to lighten your load?

Every detox serves a purpose, and there's no one-size-fits-all approach. You can also enhance your detox with herbal protocols that support the healing of specific organs (I'll list herbal protocols later in this book, but

I also recommend consulting a local herbalist or naturopathic doctor to create a custom blend).

Building Your Detox Journey: From Hydration to Deep Tissue Cleansing

If you're new to detoxing, I recommend starting simple—by focusing on hydration. Proper hydration is the foundation of any detox as it helps flush stagnation, support digestion, and optimize cellular function. Later in this book, I outline a Water Challenge Protocol, which is the first step in preparing your body for deeper cleansing. By simply increasing your intake of structured or spring water and mineralizing your hydration, you're already supporting your body's natural detox pathways.

Once you've established proper hydration, the next step is introducing a gentle cellular cleanse, such as a 24-hour to three-day juice cleanse. Juice cleanses are powerful for hydrating cells, eliminating toxins, and giving the digestive system a break. One of my favorite detox routines was doing a three-day juice cleanse on the first Wednesday of every month for six months. This allowed me to go inward and flood my body with dense, easily absorbed nutrition (unless you have severe gut inflammation—if that's the case, consult your doctor to find the best gut reset protocol).

When you're ready to go deeper, consider a seven-day to thirty-day clean-eating detox. This involves removing processed foods and inflammatory ingredients while nourishing your body with whole, clean foods. Some effective clean-eating detox protocols include:

- **Dr. Sebi's Alkaline Cleanse** – A plant-based detox that removes acidic foods to reset pH balance and eliminate mucus buildup.

- **Ayurvedic Kitchari Cleanse** – A grounding cleanse focusing on mung beans, rice, and digestive spices to deeply nourish and reset the gut.

- **Fresh Fish & Veggies Detox** – A lighter detox that includes wild-caught fish, organic vegetables, and healthy fats to support detoxification without overwhelming the system. (If you're looking for the highest-quality seafood, I personally recommend Seatopia—but always do your research, as companies evolve and change.)

The Ultimate Detox: 14-Week Deep Tissue Cleansing

The deepest detox I've ever done is Dr. Robert Morse's 14-Week Deep Tissue Cleanse and Dr. Bernard Jensen's "Ultimate Tissue Cleansing Program" (detailed in *Tissue Cleansing Through Bowel Management*).

These intense and highly transformative detox protocols require a fully alkaline diet, targeted herbal protocols, detox therapies (such as colonics, saunas, fasting, rebounding, and other biohacking techniques), and deep emotional integration. Due to their intensity, these detoxes should be done under professional guidance to monitor symptoms, as detox reactions can be significant.

Detox at Your Pace

Finishing a detox is just as important as beginning one. Reintroducing foods slowly allows you to identify sensitivities and maintain the progress you've made. Hydration remains a key part of post-detox life, as structured or spring water continues to flush out lingering toxins. The most important step, however, is integration. Detoxing isn't just about the days you cleanse—it's about how you live every day afterward. What habits will you keep? What lessons did you learn? If you don't take time to reflect and apply what you've gained, the benefits of the detox will fade. Integration is where transformation becomes permanent.

Detox Protocols
(Beginning to Advanced)

1. 3-Day Hydration Challenge: Elevate Your Energy, Mood, and Focus

Instructions:

1. Prepare Your Water
   - Fill three 1-liter glass bottles with fresh spring water (you can add key limes for natural alkalinity).
   - Set them aside for easy access throughout the day.

2. 2. Daily Drinking Schedule
   - 6 AM - 10 AM: Open the first bottle and drink as much as you can.
   - 10 AM - 2 PM: Open the second bottle and drink as much as you can.
   - 2 PM - 6 PM: Open the third bottle and drink as much as you can.

3. Track Your Progress
   - After each session, mark a line on the bottle at the water level to track how much you drank.

- At the end of the day, rinse and refill your bottles with fresh spring water.

4. Challenge Yourself
- The next day, use the previous day's line as a benchmark and try to drink more than that level.
- Repeat this process for three days, gradually increasing your hydration intake.

5. Observe the Changes
- Pay attention to shifts in your focus, mood, energy levels, and overall well-being.
- Take note of how your body responds to consistent hydration.

By the end of the Water Challenge, you may notice improved mental clarity, better digestion, and enhanced energy. Keep going and make hydration a daily habit!

2. The Master Cleanse by Stanley Burroughs

For more details, you can find Stanley Burroughs' book on Amazon. Here's how to make the cleanse:

- 2 tablespoons fresh lemon or lime juice (about ½ a lemon)
- 2 tablespoons genuine maple syrup (not maple-flavored syrup)
- 1/10 teaspoon cayenne pepper (adjust to taste)

- 8 oz room-temperature water

Shake the lemon juice, maple syrup, and cayenne pepper in a large pitcher and drink throughout the day. You can use cold water if you prefer.

Only use the highest quality ingredients: freshly squeezed lemon or lime juice, high-quality maple syrup, fresh cayenne pepper, and spring water.

Maple syrup is graded based on its mineral content and flavor:

- Grade A: A mild taste with fewer minerals; it's the first pass in the syrup-making process.
- Grade B: A stronger maple taste with more minerals.
- Grade C: The third pass, containing the highest mineral content and the most intense flavor (some find it too strong, but I'm all about that higher mineral concentration).

The mineral content of maple syrup varies depending on where the trees grow. Syrup from Vermont, for example, is rich in potassium, calcium, magnesium, manganese, iron, copper, chlorine, and silicon. It also contains vitamins A, B1, B2, B6, and C, along with nicotinic and pantothenic acids.

Be cautious—some companies use formaldehyde pellets during the sugaring process. Always research your syrup source to ensure it's pure and directly from the trees. A great brand to consider is Spring Tree from Brattleboro, Vermont (Burroughs, 2018).

3. Ayurvedic Kitchari Cleanse

If you're looking for a grounding and nourishing cleanse beyond juicing, an Ayurvedic Kitchari Cleanse is an excellent option. Kitchari is a staple in Ayurvedic detoxing, as it's gentle on digestion while providing essential nutrients to support cleansing.

Ingredients:

- ½ cup basmati rice
- 1 cup split yellow mung dal
- 6 cups water (approx.)
- ½ to 1-inch ginger root, chopped or grated
- ¼ teaspoon Celtic sea salt
- 2 teaspoons ghee

Additional Spices:

- ½ teaspoon coriander powder
- ½ teaspoon cumin powder
- ½ teaspoon whole cumin seeds
- ½ teaspoon mustard seeds
- ½ teaspoon turmeric powder

For added flavor and nutrients, garnish with fresh chopped cilantro. If desired, add steamed vegetables like zucchini, carrots, or onions.

Start by washing the rice and mung dal separately, removing any stones from the mung dal. I recommend using an Instant Pot, as it helps release gas from the beans and improves absorption. Keep in mind that the water-to-bean ratio may differ in an Instant Pot—try using 3 cups of water instead of the 6 cups suggested for stovetop cooking.

In a saucepan, heat the ghee and cook the cumin and mustard seeds until they pop. Then, add the coriander powder, cumin powder, turmeric powder, and Celtic sea salt. Mix this fragrant blend into the mung dal and rice. Finally, top it off with sautéed veggies and chopped cilantro. (Recipe adapted from The Ayurvedic Institute, 2022).

4. 14-Week Deep Tissue Cleanse

This cleanse is intense and complex, so it's crucial to work with a practitioner familiar with the program. You can find professionals by searching "14-week detox by Dr. Robert Morse" online.

The required herbal formulas are available on Dr. Morse's website at **drmorsesherbalhealthclub.com**. Since shipping times vary, it's best to call ahead to confirm availability.

As with any deep detox, you may experience a healing crisis, which can range from mild to intense. Some people have attempted this cleanse without proper guidance and ended up in the hospital, so it's essential to consult a knowledgeable practitioner.

Healing Crisis Symptoms:

- **Mild symptoms:** Headaches, body aches, flu-like symptoms, mild fever, mucus discharge (in stool or urine), fatigue, rashes, itching, weight loss, and chills.

- **Moderate symptoms:** Increased mucus discharge, darker urine, pain from old injuries, chronic fatigue, muscle spasms, diarrhea, vomiting, dizziness, heart palpitations, high fever, and skin irritation.

- **Extreme symptoms:** Severe detox reactions that require medical attention.

Dr. Robert Morse's Deep Tissue Cleanse

This cleanse is primarily fruit-based. Breakfast and lunch consist of organic fruits such as grapes (with seeds), apples, mangoes, cherries, peaches, pears, bananas, berries, and melons (which should be eaten alone).

For dinner, options include:

- More fruit
- A salad with small amounts of steamed vegetables
- Veggie soup (avoid cooked tomatoes)

- Baked sweet potatoes
- Steamed squash
- Avocado

When I followed this detox, I mainly ate fruit and supplemented with vegetables and alkaline foods from Dr. Sebi's alkaline books. While this is a general guideline, Dr. Morse's protocol is primarily fruit-based, and his book The Detox Miracle is essential reading for understanding the program in depth. Research is key before starting.

14-Week Herbal Tinctures and Supplements

Weeks 1-4:

1. Endocrine Balance
2. Lymphatic System Tonic I (capsules)
3. Kidney and Bladder Tonic I
4. Lymph Node Support II
5. Kidney and Bladder Tonic II (capsules)
6. Liver and Gallbladder Tonic
7. Parasite M
8. GI Renew

Weeks 5-10:

1. Lymph Node Support II
2. Brain and Nervous System Tonic

3. Circulation Tonic (upper body)

This stage of the detox is deep and requires commitment, but if done correctly, the benefits are transformative. It's critical to have the right support system in place.

Weeks 11-14:
1. Kidney Bladder I
2. Lymphatic System Tonic IV
3. Lymph Node Support IV
4. Lung Tonic
5. Blood Tonic
6. Adrenal Gland Tonic
7. Kidney Bladder Tonic II
8. GI Renew

During this phase, I experienced significant detox symptoms and found relief by incorporating Dr. Morse's Pain Formula and Heal All Tea.

5. Tissue Cleansing Through Bowel Management by Dr. Bernard Jensen, D.C.

This detox is more advanced and requires guidance from Dr. Bernard Jensen's book *Tissue Cleansing Through Bowel Management*. While there are countless detox programs available, these are the ones I've personally used and found to be incredibly effective.

Each cleanse offers different benefits and levels of intensity. Whether you start with a simple juice cleanse, an Ayurvedic Kitchari detox, or a deep tissue protocol, the most important part of detoxing is listening to your body. Detoxification is not just about eliminating toxins—it's about resetting your body, mind, and spirit to function at their highest potential.

Hacking Your Detox and Taking It to the Next Level

Scan the QR code below to fill out a quick form (I promise—no spam!), and I'll email you my *Thoughtwork Workbook*. This workbook includes journal prompts designed to help you explore deeper self-awareness and support you through any detox—whether emotional, physical, or spiritual.

CHAPTER 8

Plant Medicine and Psychedelics for Mental Health

My Journey with Psychedelics and Mental Health

In 2023, I completed my Master's in Psychology with a focus on coaching. From the beginning of my program, I made a conscious decision: whenever I had the chance to choose a research topic, I would dive into the science-backed evidence surrounding psychedelics and mental health. I expected my papers to stir some controversy, but the reality was quite the opposite—my professors embraced them, and I loved every moment of the learning process.

However, my interest in psilocybin for depression began long before my academic research. For much of my life, I struggled with severe depression and unexplained health issues. As you've read, I detoxed extensively—again and again—yet something still wasn't clicking. Detoxing got me closer to my emotional and physical goals, but I still faced deep, debilitating lows. There were moments when I didn't want to be here anymore, and that terrified me. But perhaps that very fear pushed me to continue searching—to truly crack the code of healing depression.

I started microdosing psilocybin because I've never been comfortable losing control, and the thought of a full psychedelic experience terrified me. The idea of encountering something beyond my control was overwhelming. For years, I experimented with microdosing, carefully adjusting the dosage but never leaning into a full, heroic dose. I knew that if I were ever to take that leap, I'd need someone who could hold space for PTSD, depression, and grief with deep knowledge and tenderness. From personal experience, I knew that not many people truly understand how to do that.

One of my most profound realizations came from a traumatic experience with a well-known hypnotherapist. She helped me uncover a deeply buried trauma—something I had always sensed but had suppressed so deeply that it remained locked in my subconscious. The session brought it to the surface, but rather than guiding me as an observer, she placed me directly inside the trauma. I relived every moment, completely raw and unguarded. Overwhelmed and hysterical, I wasn't led toward resolution. The session ended abruptly. She told me my time was up, moved me to a plastic chair in the hallway, and began preparing for her next client. Shaking and sobbing uncontrollably, I stumbled to my car, where I continued to cry alone.

That moment changed me. It was the catalyst that led me to study hypnotherapy myself—not just to understand trauma, but to ensure no one I worked with would ever be left in that vulnerable state without support. In my practice, I intentionally leave generous time between clients for this very reason. Sometimes, experiencing something extreme teaches us how to better help others.

After that, I sought therapy, but financial constraints made it inaccessible. So, I turned to what I could afford—psilocybin. I began macrodosing, which allowed me to maintain control while also creating space to process my own pain. I don't recommend this path alone, but at the time, it was the best I could do as a mother of three young children.

Each time I microdosed, my mind felt noticeably clearer the next day. It was working—but only to a point. I still struggled with depression and deep grief when I was alone. Through my master's research, I also explored the therapeutic effects of ketamine and MDMA, both of which showed promising results for depression and anxiety. I wanted to try them, but I was cautious about the risks of using street versions of these substances. So, I waited until I had access to high-quality, doctor-prescribed ketamine and MDMA in a safe, controlled environment.

When the time came, I started with MDMA. The experience was profound—my heart expanded, and I remembered what love felt like. Every cell in my body recalled that sensation. As humans, we are often disconnected from this feeling. We are taught to hustle—pay bills, rush through life, and survive. We aren't taught to slow down, connect, integrate, and create. As a society, we are deeply disconnected. It's time to remember—to feel what it's like to be loved and to embody love itself.

As the MDMA effects faded, I moved on to ketamine. With ketamine, I became an observer of myself. It was as though I saw my life without the filters of conditioning, trauma, or self-perception. And in that space, I discovered my deepest truth: I was love, and I was never truly alone in this world.

That was my core wound.

I had spent my life feeling unloved and alone, and until that moment, no detox, therapy, or coaching had reached the depth of that pain. But there, in that experience, it healed. From that day forward, I no longer felt disconnected or unloved. I felt an unwavering connection to myself, my purpose, and my place in the world.

This changed everything for me.

For me, psilocybin helped me work through many layers, but it didn't take me to my core wound. Perhaps that was the path I needed—I had to unravel the pieces before I could reach and heal the deepest layer.

Since that experience, I haven't felt the need to return to those substances. I'm curious about what other layers I may uncover in the future, but for now, I feel complete. I now understand the profound importance of psychedelics—not as a magic cure, but as a tool. For me, they provided access to a part of myself that no therapist, coach, or detox had been able to touch.

Psychedelics aren't the answer for everyone, but they are an option.

For those interested in the scientific protocols and significant research findings on psychedelics for depression and anxiety, I'll include additional resources at the end of this book.

Authenticate Your Life: Expanded Chapters

After *Authenticate Your Life* was published, the journey doesn't end—there will always be more to explore. As of February 25, 2025, I'm beginning my second book, but in the meantime, I'll be sharing additional chapters on my website, which you can access by scanning this QR code.

The first extended chapter takes a deeper dive into psychedelics for mental health. Just last week, I explored ketamine for the first time, and I have a lot to share. In short, it pulled my nervous system out of a freeze state and into peace for an hour and a half. Since then, I've felt a profound shift—moving out of depression and back into flow.

For the full experience and insights, scan here:

Conclusion: Coming Home to Yourself

Throughout this book, we've explored the layers of authenticity—what it means to strip away conditioning, break free from limiting patterns, and fully step into the life that feels most aligned with who you truly are.

The journey to authentic living is not a straight path. It's a spiral—one that brings you back to yourself over and over again, revealing deeper layers of healing, truth, and alignment. It's about learning to trust your intuition, listen to your body, and honor the wisdom that has always been within you.

For me, this journey was not about finding something external to validate my existence. It was about remembering. Remembering that I am already whole. That I am not here to fit into someone else's mold, but to fully embrace my own unique frequency. Authenticity isn't about perfection—it's about presence. It's about living in alignment with what feels true, not what looks good from the outside.

I have walked through grief, trauma, loss, and deep transformation. I've detoxed my body, rewired my subconscious, and tested the edges of my own healing—always searching for the key that would unlock a life free from depression, anxiety, and old survival patterns. And what I discovered is that the key was never outside of me. It was always in the space where I allowed myself to feel, to remember, and to reclaim my power.

Authenticity isn't about what you do. It's about how you be. It's the energy you carry, the presence you embody, and the truth you stand in. It's about making choices that nourish your mind, body, and soul instead of those that keep you stuck in a cycle of depletion and self-abandonment.

There is no final destination in this work—only deeper levels of freedom, alignment, and self-awareness. But I promise you this: the more you choose authenticity, the more life meets you with magic. Doors open. Healing accelerates. The right people and opportunities find you—not because you force them, but because you are finally aligned with them.

So, as you close this book, I invite you to take a deep breath and ask yourself:

Who am I when I am fully free?

What is one small shift I can make today that aligns me more deeply with my truth?

What would it feel like to trust my own wisdom, fully and completely?

You are here for a reason. You are already enough. And the life you desire—the one that feels like home—is waiting for you on the other side of your courage.

All you have to do is step into it.

With love,
Cori

About the Author

Cori Roberts has always been ahead of her time. Her passion for holistic healing and transformation began after the birth of her second child, when she launched her first business, *Holistic Waters*, offering colon hydrotherapy. This introduction to detoxification led her to study the groundbreaking work of Dr. Bernard Jensen, a pioneer in bowel cleansing and tissue detoxification. She worked with the Colenz system—developed in collaboration with Dr. Jensen—which sparked her deep dive into probiotics, gut health, infrared saunas, hypnotherapy, and Dr. Robert Morse's advanced detox protocols.

As Cori expanded her expertise beyond colon hydrotherapy to include coaching, hypnosis, trauma-informed therapy, and energy healing, she came to understand that true transformation requires a mind-body-spirit approach. Over time, her work evolved from focusing on the gut to helping individuals heal from the inside out—bridging physical health with emotional and energetic alignment.

Education & Certifications

Cori holds a master's degree in psychology with an emphasis on coaching from Grand Canyon University. She is a certified hypnotherapist, trained in Dolores Cannon's Quantum Healing Hypnosis Technique (QHHT) and SWIHA's Hypnotherapy Certification Program. Additionally, Cori is a detox expert and trauma-aware life coach. Her multidisciplinary background allows her to integrate psychology, holistic wellness, and intuitive healing into her work with individuals and businesses.

What's Next?

Cori is now expanding her work beyond one-on-one coaching into community-based detox programs, retreats, and transformational healing experiences.

Detox Membership Programs (Now Open!)

- A guided, supportive space for individuals looking to deepen their detox journey, heal their bodies, and transform their lives.
- Includes access to live coaching, detox protocols, Q&A sessions, exclusive resources, and a supportive community.
- Visit coriroberts.com to join!

1:1 Transformational Coaching (Available Now!)

- 60-minute personalized coaching sessions with Cori to support you in healing, detoxing, and aligning with your highest self.
- Whether you're navigating a major life transition, working through emotional blockages, or looking for deep detox support, Cori offers intuitive, science-backed guidance.
- Book a session at coriroberts.com.

Coming Soon: Mind-Body-Spirit Reset Retreats

- In-person wellness retreats focused on deep detox, emotional release, nervous system healing, and spiritual renewal.

- Includes organic meals, guided healing sessions, nature immersion, movement practices, and transformational coaching.
- Stay tuned for details and retreat dates!

Connect with Cori

For more information about Cori and her work, visit **coriroberts.com** or follow her on social media at **Words2Wellness**. Whether you're just starting your detox journey or looking for advanced support in healing and transformation, Cori's mission is to help you clear the blocks, align your energy, and step into your most powerful, authentic self.

Resources

Throughout my journey, I've encountered incredible books, podcasts, and thought leaders who have shaped my understanding of detox, healing, and personal transformation. These resources have been instrumental in helping me deepen my knowledge and refine my practices, and I'm excited to share them with you. Whether you're just starting out or diving deeper into detox and personal growth, these books, podcasts, and experts will provide invaluable guidance.

Books That Transformed My Approach to Healing

The Detox Miracle Source Book by Dr. Robert Morse – This book is an absolute must-read if you're serious about detox. Dr. Morse explains the body's functions in a clear and accessible way, connecting everything to cellular regeneration and detoxification. He dives deep into raw foods, herbs, and the body's natural healing processes, making this one of the most valuable resources I've used. I highly recommend checking out pages 264-271, where he outlines key detox protocols.

Tissue Cleansing Through Bowel Management by Bernard Jensen – This book changed everything for me. Dr. Jensen was one of the pioneers of bowel and tissue cleansing, and his book provides a comprehensive look at detoxification and gut health. His Ultimate Tissue Cleansing protocol is one of the most intense bowel and tissue cleanses I've ever done. Written in 1981, the wisdom in this book remains as relevant today as ever, proving that detoxing is not a trend but an ancient healing practice.

Heal Your Life by Louise Hay – First published in 1984, this book is essential for understanding the connection between the emotional and physical body. It offers a simple yet powerful dictionary linking emotions to specific areas of the body, helping you see how unresolved trauma and emotional blockages might affect your health. I've referenced this book countless times over the years, and it's a staple in my personal library.

Podcasts & Thought Leaders That Shifted My Perspective

Zach Bush – Dr. Zach Bush's work has been a huge source of inspiration for me. His transition from the traditional medical field to becoming a leader in regenerative agriculture, gut health, and the microbiome has been incredible to witness. His insights into the connection between soil health and human health completely transformed how I view detox, nutrition, and overall well-being.

Luke Storey & Dave Asprey – If you're into biohacking, optimizing your body's natural processes, and discovering new ways to improve health, these two are game-changers. Luke Storey and Dave Asprey are at the forefront of cutting-edge wellness technology, anti-aging strategies, and detoxification methods. Their research and experiments have influenced the way I approach deep detox, hydration, and nervous system regulation.

Abraham Hicks – If you want to reclaim your power and start manifesting the life you desire, Abraham Hicks' teachings are a must. Her work on the law of attraction, energy alignment, and conscious creation has deeply impacted my journey. She helped me understand that we are the creators of our reality, and that the thoughts and emotions we hold shape our experiences.

Joe Dispenza – Dr. Joe Dispenza's work has been a major influence on my understanding of the mind-body connection and the power of meditation to transform health. His research-backed approach shows that rewiring the subconscious mind through meditation can lead to real, lasting physical healing. If you've ever questioned whether your thoughts and emotions impact your body, his books, meditations, and teachings will provide the proof.

Joe Rogan Podcast #1035 with Paul Stamets – This episode was a turning point for me. It opened my eyes to the potential of psilocybin (magic mushrooms) for mental health and trauma healing. The discussion on how psychedelics can support PTSD, depression, and anxiety recovery was so powerful that it led me to further explore the role of plant medicine, ketamine, and MDMA therapy in healing.

Gregg Braden's Podcast & Teachings – Gregg Braden is a scientist, author, and researcher who bridges the gap between science, spirituality, and human potential. His work focuses on the power of our hearts, the intelligence of our DNA, and how ancient wisdom aligns with modern physics. His research validates what many of us have known intuitively—that our thoughts, emotions, and beliefs directly impact our biology and environment.

Andrew Huberman – A neuroscientist and professor at Stanford University, Dr. Huberman's podcast, *Huberman Lab*, dives deep into the science of human performance, brain function, and optimal health. His research on sleep, stress, neuroplasticity, and nervous system regulation has completely transformed how I approach recovery and peak performance.

Robert Edward Grant – A true visionary, Grant explores the intersections of mathematics, sacred geometry, and consciousness. His work offers deep insights into the codes of the universe, ancient knowledge, and how numerical patterns influence our lives.

Peter Crone – Known as *The Mind Architect*, Peter Crone specializes in reprogramming subconscious limitations, breaking free from mental conditioning, and stepping into personal freedom.

Mastin Kipp – A leader in emotional trauma healing and purpose-driven living, Mastin's work focuses on helping individuals turn their past wounds into wisdom.

Matthias J Barker – Matthias is a therapist and speaker who explores emotional resilience, trauma healing, and personal growth. His ability to break down complex psychological concepts into relatable, practical insights makes his podcast a great resource for anyone looking to deepen their self-awareness and emotional intelligence.

Dr. Frank Anderson – A psychiatrist and trauma expert, Dr. Anderson is at the forefront of Internal Family Systems (IFS) therapy and healing childhood trauma. His work focuses on helping people understand, heal, and integrate the different parts of themselves—something I talk about often in this book. His approach blends science, spirituality, and deep emotional work, making him a must-follow for anyone seeking to heal deeply rooted wounds.

Final Thoughts

The more we learn, the more we realize how much we don't know. Healing is a lifelong journey of unlearning old patterns, reconnecting with ourselves, and discovering what truly aligns with our highest good.

I hope these resources help you as much as they've helped me. If you ever feel stuck, remember—you have the power to transform your life. It all starts from within.

With love and healing,

Cori Roberts

REFERENCES

Burroughs, S. (2018). *The Master Cleanse by Stanley Burroughs.* Independently published.

Jensen, B., D.C. (1980). *Tissue Cleansing Through Bowel Management*. B. Jensen, 1981. [Bernard Jensen](https://bernardj.com/about-us/)

Morse, R. (2013). *The Detox Miracle Sourcebook: Raw Foods and Herbs for Complete Cellular Regeneration: The Ultimate Healing System.* (p.104) Hohm Press, U.S. [Dr. Morse's Herbal Health Club](https://drmorsesherbalhealthclub.com)

The Ayurvedic Institute. (2022, September 12). *Kitchari.* *Ayurveda.* [The Ayurvedic Institute](https://www.ayurveda.com/recipes-kitchari/)

Vermes, K. (2020, March 17). *All about the Chinese body clock*. Healthline. https://www.healthline.com/health/chinese-body-clock

Yehuda, R., Daskalakis, N., Bierera, L., Klengel, T., & Holsboer, F. (2015). Holocaust exposure induced intergenerational effects on FKBP5 methylation. *Biological Psychiatry Journal, 80*(5). https://doi.org/10.1016/j.biopsych.2015.08.005

Here are some of the best websites for researchers to find reliable statistical data on psychedelics and their effects on depression and anxiety:

Academic & Research Databases

1. PubMed — A leading source for peer-reviewed medical and psychological research, including studies on psychedelics.
2. Google Scholar — A broad academic search engine that includes studies, citations, and meta-analyses from various journals and institutions.
3. PsycINFO (APA Database) — A database of psychological research, including studies on psychedelics, depression, and anxiety.
4. ScienceDirect — A large database of research articles in the life sciences and health fields, including psychedelic research.

Psychedelic Research Organizations & Institutes

5. Multidisciplinary Association for Psychedelic Studies (MAPS) — One of the leading organizations funding research on psychedelics, including clinical trials for depression and PTSD.
6. Johns Hopkins Center for Psychedelic & Consciousness Research — One of the foremost institutions studying psilocybin and its effects on mental health.
7. Imperial College London Psychedelic Research Centre — Conducts cutting-edge research on psychedelics and their therapeutic potential.

8. UC Berkeley Center for the Science of Psychedelics — Focuses on rigorous scientific research into the effects of psychedelics on mental health.
9. Heffter Research Institute — A nonprofit dedicated to funding scientific research on classic psychedelics, particularly psilocybin.
10. The Beckley Foundation — A research institution that studies the impact of psychedelics on consciousness and mental health.

Government & Health Agencies

11. National Institute on Drug Abuse (NIDA) — Provides data on psychedelics, addiction research, and clinical trials.
12. ClinicalTrials.gov — Lists ongoing and completed clinical trials related to psychedelics, depression, and anxiety.
13. World Health Organization (WHO) — Publishes reports on mental health, substance use, and global psychedelic research efforts.
14. Centers for Disease Control and Prevention (CDC) — Provides statistics on mental health and substance use trends, including psychedelic use.

Additional Resources

15. Erowid — A community-driven resource with reports on subjective experiences and scientific studies on psychedelics.
16. Psychedelic Science Review — Features research articles and scientific reviews on psychedelics and mental health.

17. Open Science Framework (OSF) — A platform where researchers share data, preprints, and study findings on psychedelics.
18. PsyPost — Covers the latest psychological research, including psychedelic therapy studies.

Throughout this section, we've explored various methods to recharge and optimize your Life Force Energy (LFE). Here's a summary of the key practices:

1. Biohacking Technologies

- PEMF Therapy (Pulsed Electromagnetic Field Machines) – Recharges cellular energy like a battery.
- BioCharger – Uses frequencies to enhance overall health and detoxification.
- Harmonic Egg & Rife Machines – Utilizes sound and electromagnetic frequencies for healing.
- Infrared Saunas – Supports detoxification, circulation, and deep relaxation.
- Mini Theragun & Vibration Plate (LifePro Waver Mini) – Stimulates the lymphatic system and relieves tension.

2. Sleep & Circadian Rhythm Alignment

- Prioritizing deep, restorative sleep to allow the body to heal.
- Understanding the Traditional Chinese Medicine (TCM) Organ Clock to optimize sleep and organ function.

- Using wearable sleep trackers (e.g., Whoop band) to monitor sleep quality.

3. Grounding & Nature Connection
- Walking barefoot (Earthing) to absorb Earth's natural energy.
- Spending time in green spaces, forests, jungles, or by bodies of water to recharge.

4. Breathwork & Meditation
- Square Breathing and other breathwork techniques to calm the nervous system.
- Mindfulness meditation to clear mental clutter and enhance presence.

5. Hydration & High-Vibrational Nutrition
- Drinking structured or mineral-rich water to optimize cellular hydration.
- Consuming high-energy, whole foods.

6. Movement & Exercise (Tailored to Your Energy Needs)
- Gentle movement for chronic illness – Walking, stretching, light yoga.
- Strength & cardio – If it genuinely energizes you rather than depletes you.

7. Energy Healing & Bodywork

- Massage, craniosacral therapy, polarity therapy, reflexology, and acupuncture to release stored tension.

8. Emotional Release & Mental Health Support

- Seeking trauma-informed therapists, hypnotherapists, or transformational coaches.
- Journaling, creative expression, or talk therapy to process emotions.

9. Intimacy & Connection

- Deep connection with a partner – through touch, communication, and vulnerability.
- Solo self-care – such as baths, self-massage, or personal reflection.

10. Identifying Energy Drains & Protecting Your LFE

- Evaluating activities, people, and environments that either increase or deplete your energy.
- Setting energetic boundaries and consciously choosing where to invest your time and attention.

www.ingramcontent.com/pod-product-compliance
Lightning Source LLC
Chambersburg PA
CBHW030449100526
44580CB00002B/48